Dedication

To my husband, Don, who has stood by my side for over a decade, through the weight of trauma I often struggled to carry. Your unwavering support has been my anchor.

To my children, whose love and laughter remind me every day to strive for the best version of myself. You are my greatest inspiration.

To my Godmother, my confidante, my therapist in the shadows, my crisis line when the past tries to break through. You realign me when I lose my way, and for that, I am forever grateful.

To my Pastor Paul Kelker, whose guidance has strengthened my faith and reminded me that my healing is in my hands.

And most importantly, to every child who has ever felt unheard—your voice matters.

PRELUDE

The roar of the 405 Freeway was the constant backdrop of my childhood, a relentless hum that seeped through the thin walls of our three-bedroom apartment on the westside of Los Angeles. It wasn't much, but it was home—just me, my dad, and my older brother, Jerome Jr., or JJ as everyone called him. At twelve, JJ was seven years my senior, a gap wide enough to make him my protector, tormentor, and occasional teacher all rolled into one.

Life was simple, in a way. Days were marked by the rhythm of school, homework, and the ever-present hum of the freeway. My dad worked long hours at his construction job, coming home exhausted but always present in his own quiet way. JJ, when he wasn't at school, was usually out with friends, leaving me to my own devices. I spent hours lost in my imagination, creating worlds and characters to fill the silence of our small apartment.

But our small world was about to change. My dad, a man who had always shied away from commitment, announced he was getting married. Barbara, his fiancée, was a whirlwind of energy and opinions, a stark contrast to the quiet routine we were used to. She moved in with us, bringing a suitcase full of brightly colored clothes and a determination to turn our apartment into a home.

I watched them—my dad and Barbara—with a mixture of curiosity and apprehension. They were happy, their laughter echoing through the apartment, their hands always intertwined. But their happiness felt distant, like a scene playing out on a television screen, something I could observe but never quite participate in.

It wasnt just us, not entirely. I had a sister, Jamie, just twenty-two days younger than me. But Jamie lived with her mother, a woman who had spent years struggling with addiction. Her life was a chaotic mess of bad choices and broken promises at one point. I watched them—Jamie and her mother—and felt a pang of sadness. I knew Jamie's life was a glimpse into what mine could have been, had my own mother not succumbed to the same demons that once haunted Jamie's mother. The difference? Jamie's mother fought her demons until she won for the sake of her love for her daughter.

My dad, a man of few words and even fewer emotions, had rescued me from my fate. He had driven to Riverside, where I had been living with my grandmother, and brought me home. He didn't talk about it much, but I knew he had saved me. He had given me a chance at a different life, a life free from the chaos and despair that had consumed my mother.

But even with my dad's love and Barbara's attempts to create a sense of normalcy, I couldn't shake the feeling that something was missing. I longed for connection, for a sense of belonging that always seemed just out of reach. I watched the other children at school, their easy friendships and carefree laughter, and felt a pang of envy. I wanted what they had—the simple joy of being a child—but the darkness, it clung to me, the legacy of my mother's addiction, and the ever-present tension of JJ's unpredictable moods kept me on the outside, a solitary figure in a world that seemed to have no place for me.

CHAPTER 1: The Wedding That Sealed Our Fate

The wedding was a blur of lace, gold, and forced smiles. I stood beside Jamie, my half-sister, our matching pink dresses itchy against our skin. We weren't twins, but we might as well have been. Two little girls standing side by side, waiting for someone to tell us what to do.

"Hold the basket like this, baby," one of the older women instructed, adjusting my grip on the petals.

I nodded but said nothing. I didn't care about the flowers.

I cared that this moment meant Barbara wasn't leaving. She had already been living with us for months, her perfume settling into the walls, her voice weaving itself into our daily lives. But now, with the rings exchanged and the papers signed, it felt final.

Before, there had been a tiny hope—a sliver of a chance that she might leave. That things would go back to normal.

But now, normal was gone.

The ceremony moved in slow motion, words I didn't understand floating around me as my dad and Barbara promised forever. I watched them, my dad in an ill-fitting suit, Barbara glowing in her white gown, and I felt... nothing.

Not happiness. Not sadness. Just... nothing.

At the reception, the world became a blur of loud music, strange food, and unfamiliar hands patting my head.

I stayed glued to Jamie's side, both of us watching from the edges as the adults danced, drank, and laughed louder than usual.

Barbara was spinning in her dress, smiling so wide her teeth gleamed under the dim lights.

I wanted to believe that this was a happy ending, that Barbara would make our home warm, that love would settle into the walls.

But deep down, I already knew better.

I could feel it in the way JJ sat alone in the corner, his expression unreadable.

I could see it in the way my dad's laughter didn't quite reach his eyes.

And later that night, I would see it in the way JJ stood in my doorway.

CHAPTER 2: JJ'S FAVORITE GAME

The house was dark when we got home.

Barbara was still floating on her wedding high, Dad a little looser than usual, and for a moment, it almost felt safe.

But then the night settled in. I had just climbed into bed, wrapping myself in the sheets, when I heard it—

The door creaking open. I didn't have to look. I already knew who it was.

JJ's shadow stretched across the floor, swallowing the space between us. He stood there, just watching.

Watching like he always did.

Then, in a voice so low it barely cut through the silence, he said the words that sent a chill down my spine.

"You know what to do."

And just like that, the wedding, the happiness, the tiny sliver of hope I had held onto…

Vanished.

Because this wasn't a home. It was a cage.

And JJ was the lock.

The silence in the room was suffocating, thick like fog, pressing against my skin.

JJ didn't move right away. He just stood there, watching. His silhouette stretched across the floor, the glow from the hallway casting his shadow long and ominous, like a monster creeping into my world.

I held my breath. Maybe if I didn't move, didn't breathe, he would leave. Maybe tonight, he would change the rules.

But JJ never changed the rules.

He stepped inside, closing the door behind him with the softest click. The kind that sent chills down my spine because I knew what it meant. No one would hear me. No one ever did.

He didn't have to say it again. I already knew what he wanted. I knew what he expected.

Because JJ loved power.

And fear was his favorite game.

He didn't have to hit me. He didn't have to raise his voice. All he had to do was look at me a certain way. The way he stood too close.

The way his lips curled into a slow smirk, like he knew something I didn't.

The way his voice dipped so low, it made my stomach twist in knots.

"You know no one wants you, right?" His voice was calm, almost casual. Like he was stating a fact, not trying to break me into smaller pieces.

I swallowed hard, staring at the wall.

It wasn't true. I told myself that, again and again, it wasn't true.

But part of me believed him.

Because no one ever came.

No one ever checked.

No one ever asked.

And if they did, they never listened.

CHAPTER 3: THE PRICE OF SILENCE

The next morning, I moved through the house like a ghost. My body was here, going through the motions—getting dressed, eating breakfast, packing my school bag—but my mind was somewhere else. Somewhere outside my skin, drifting between memories I wanted to forget and the ones I couldn't escape.

Dad barely looked up from his coffee as I slipped into the kitchen.

Barbara was humming to herself, stirring sugar into her cup, oblivious to the way my hands shook as I reached for a spoon.

And JJ?

JJ was sitting at the table, chewing his cereal like he hadn't shattered my world just hours before.

Like nothing had happened.

Like nothing ever happened.

I wanted to scream. To throw the bowl of cereal across the room. To make someone notice.

But instead, I stirred my oatmeal in silence.

At school, the air felt lighter. Safer.

I clung to that, the illusion of normal.

I lost myself in math problems, letting the numbers block out the noise in my head.

But when lunchtime came, I wasn't hungry. The cafeteria was loud, too loud, and the smell of food made my stomach turn.

I found my usual spot outside, near the chain-link fence, where no one would bother me.

I picked at the hem of my sleeve, my fingers tracing the tiny bruises just beneath the fabric. Dark spots in the shape of fingertips.

I pulled my sleeve down, forcing myself to focus on the sky instead.

The sun was shining. The world was still moving.

But inside, I felt like I was disappearing.

CHAPTER 4: WHEN I TRIED TO TELL

Ms. Smith noticed. She always did.

She had a way of seeing through me, like she knew the weight I carried even when I tried to hide it.

"Tess," she said gently as the class emptied out for recess. "Can you stay for a second?"

My stomach twisted. Had I done something wrong?

I nodded and sat frozen in my chair as she crouched beside my desk.

"Are you feeling okay?" she asked. "You've seemed… quiet."

Quiet.

I almost laughed. If only she knew. I stared at my hands, my fingers curling into fists in my lap.

"I'm fine," I whispered.

Ms. Smith didn't look convinced. "Are you sure? Because if something's wrong, you can tell me. I won't be mad. I just want to help."

I wanted to tell her.

The words sat heavy on my tongue, but I couldn't push them out.

JJ's voice echoed in my head:

"You know what happens if you tell."

And suddenly, my throat was too tight. My hands were sweaty. My heart was racing so fast it hurt.

If I told, he'd know.

And if he knew, he'd make me regret it.

So I shook my head. Forced a smile. Pretended everything was fine.

Ms. Smith studied me for a moment, then sighed.

"Okay," she said softly. "But if you ever need to talk… I'm here."

I nodded quickly and bolted out of the room, my heart pounding.

Because I knew the truth.

No one could save me.

CHAPTER 5: STEALING FOR JJ

The first time JJ made me steal from Dad, I almost got caught.

I still remember the way my hands shook as I slid open the drawer.

The creak of wood was loud in the silence.

I held my breath. Waited.

Dad stirred in his sleep, letting out a low sigh.

I stood frozen, my fingers hovering over his wallet.

JJ's rules were clear.

Two bills, leave it alone.

Three bills, take one.

Four bills, take two.

That night, there were four twenties.

I took two as instructed.

My breath caught as I slid the drawer shut, every tiny sound feeling like a gunshot in the silence.

I stood there for a second, watching Dad's chest rise and fall.

Then, with silent steps, I slipped out of the room.

Back in our bedroom, JJ was already awake.
Sitting up. Waiting.
I placed the money in his hand.
He counted it quickly, his face twisting in disappointment.
"That's it?" he hissed.
I nodded, my throat tight.
"There … there wasn't more I could take."
JJ scoffed, shaking his head.
"Next time, don't come back with so little."
Then he rolled over and pulled the blanket over his head, like I wasn't even there.
Like I didn't just risk everything for him.
I climbed into my bed, curling into myself.
My hands still smelled like Dad's wallet.
And I felt sick.

Home wasn't a place of comfort.
It was a war zone.
Every step I took, every word I spoke, felt like walking through a minefield.
JJ's laughter echoed through the apartment, but it wasn't warm or friendly. It was sharp. Cold. Like a knife being sharpened.

I kept my head down. Stayed out of the way.

But it was never enough.

In this house, silence wasn't safety.

It was survival.

CHAPTER 6: A WHISPER OF TRUTH

The next morning, I woke up exhausted, as if I hadn't slept at all. My body felt heavy, my mind clouded, but I got up anyway. There was no choice. JJ's words from the night before still echoed in my ears: "Next time, don't come back with so little."

In the kitchen, the smell of burnt toast lingered. My dad was sitting at the table, his face buried in the morning paper, but I noticed the tension in his shoulders. He wasn't just reading—he was thinking. I could tell by the way he tapped his finger against the table, a slow, repetitive rhythm.

"Barbara," he said, not looking up, "have you seen any money laying around? Something funny occurred I am missing a few bills that I thought I had last night."

Barbara, busy stirring instant coffee, paused for just a second before shaking her head. "No," she said casually. "I haven't touched it. Maybe you spent it yesterday and forgot?"

My dad muttered something under his breath, brushing it off for the moment. But his gaze shifted toward me, and for a brief second, I held my breath. He didn't say anything, though. He just turned back to his paper, leaving the question hanging in the air. I grabbed my backpack and slipped out of the kitchen as quickly as I could.

At school, I tried to focus. Numbers and letters on the chalkboard were easier to deal with than anything waiting for me at home. Math especially gave me a small sense of control. It had rules, patterns, answers. Unlike my life, where everything felt unpredictable and dangerous.

But even though I did well in my studies, I struggled everywhere else. The other kids whispered when I wasn't looking, their laughter sometimes louder than the teacher's voice. They didn't understand me, and I didn't understand them. I talked too much, cried too much, and acted out when I felt the walls closing in on me. I wasn't like them. I wasn't carefree or lighthearted. How could I be, when my five-year-old body was being battered and bruised more than any grown mans that I knew?

As always, during recess, I sat alone by the fence, running my fingers over the faint bruises on my arm. I pulled my sleeve down quickly when one of the teachers on duty walked by, forcing a smile that I hoped looked real. The truth was, I didn't want anyone to see, and at the same time, I desperately wanted someone to notice. Back in class, Ms. Smith, my first-grade teacher, gave me a concerned look as I fidgeted at my desk. She was stern but fair, the kind of teacher who didn't tolerate nonsense but had a way of making you feel seen. I liked her, even when I got in trouble, because she was the closest thing I had to someone who really understood me.

After class, while the other kids rushed out to lunch, I stayed behind. Ms. Smith was erasing the chalkboard, her back to me, but she must have sensed I wasn't leaving.

"Everything okay, Tess?" she asked, turning around.

I hesitated. The words sat heavy on my tongue, tangled with fear and doubt. If I told her, would she believe me? Would she even be able to help? I opened my mouth, closed it again, and then finally said, "My brother hits me."

The piece of chalk she was holding slipped from her hand, falling to the floor with a soft thud. Her face changed instantly, her sharp expression softening into something more tender—concern, maybe even fear.

She walked over and crouched down to my level, her eyes searching mine.

"What did you say?" she asked gently, her voice barely above a whisper.

I hesitated again, my heart racing. I felt like I had just opened a door I couldn't close. "JJ hits me," I said, my voice trembling now. "He hits me a lot."

Ms. Smith stayed quiet for a moment, her lips pressing into a thin line. She looked like she was deciding something, weighing the words I'd just said. Finally, she spoke. "Tess, thank you for telling me. You're very brave."

The word brave stuck in my head, but I didn't feel brave. I felt scared. Scared of what would happen if JJ found out I told. Scared of what might happen if no one believed me. Scared of everything.

Ms. Smith told me to go to lunch and promised we'd talk more later. I left the classroom with my heart pounding, the weight of my confession pressing down on me. I didn't know what was going to happen next, but I knew one thing for sure: I couldn't take back what I had said. For the first time, someone knew.

CHAPTER 7: A NAME THAT WASNT MINE

Ms. Smith didn't mention my confession again for the rest of the day. For the time being, I was left to sit with my words, the weight of them pressing against my chest like a secret I both regretted sharing and longed to have someone understand.

When I got home, I did my homework quietly at the kitchen table. The apartment felt unusually still, like it was holding its breath. My stepmother hummed softly from the kitchen, her movements deliberate as she cleaned the counters. JJ was somewhere in the apartment, his presence a shadow lurking in the background, and I made it a point to stay out of his way. My dad wasn't home yet, and a part of me hoped he'd stay out late.

The phone rang, shattering the fragile peace. My stepmother handed it to me. "It's your grandma," she said, already turning away.

It was my mom's mom. Grandma. She was the one who had taken in all of my mother's children during her addiction, raising them when my mom couldn't.

"Hi, Grandma," I said softly.

"Hi, Teresa," she replied warmly, the name cutting through me like a blade. I hated that name.

My mom had six children, and I was the youngest. All of their names were powerful, almost poetic—Love, Beauty, Power, Fortune, and Majesty. And then there was me: Teresa. A name that didn't belong, a name that felt plain and out of place among them. It was a burden no one else could understand.

The story behind my name only made it worse. I wasn't supposed to stay with my family. My grandma couldn't take in another child—she was already raising my mother's five other kids and was growing older, tired. I was supposed to be given away to one of her friends, a trade-off meant to lighten her load. The deal was that the woman who was supposed to take me got to name me. And she did. Teresa.

But the adoption never happened, and my dad eventually came to get me. Yet the name stuck, a constant reminder of how close I'd come to being given away, to being set apart from everyone else. So I changed it. I started calling myself Tess, a name that felt sharper, stronger, and most importantly, mine. Tess was my way of reclaiming my identity. It was my way of saying, "Even if I didn't control how I came into this world, I could control who I became."

Even as a little girl, I understood that I didn't want to carry the weight of being the one who didn't belong. I didn't want to see myself as the unwanted one. But no matter how hard I tried, the truth lingered. I was the only one raised apart from my siblings. And even in the home I grew up in, the sibling I lived with—JJ—hated me. My existence felt like a mistake no one wanted to claim.

Still, the conversation with my grandma went well. We talked about school, about my siblings and what they were up to and about my upcoming summer visit. Her voice was warm, familiar, and steady, even though it carried the weight of a woman who had already done more than her share of raising children.

She told me about Fortune, the sister closest in age to me. Fortune was in cheerleading now and on the church's praise dance team. I forced a smile as she talked, but inside, I felt the familiar sting of resentment. I hated Fortune. She was the sister right above me, and she had a way of making sure I always felt like I didn't belong.

Whenever Majesty, my older brother, was around, the two of them would gang up on me. They'd whisper and giggle, calling me the adopted one, saying I wasn't really family. Their words cut deep, even though I tried not to let them see it. Fortune had a perfect name, a perfect life, and a perfect place in the family. Meanwhile, I was just... Teresa. Or at least that's how they made me feel. And yet, despite how Fortune and Majesty treated me during summer visits, those months brought a kind of relief I couldn't find anywhere else. Even though I was picked on, I was safe. I didn't have to steal, and I didn't have to live in fear of JJ's punishments. I may have been the outsider to my siblings, but my grandma loved me. She never made me feel unwanted. And for one season every year, my bruises got a chance to heal. When the summer ended, I would return to my dad's house, to the life that felt like a warzone. But for those fleeting months at Grandma's, I could breathe. I could exist without feeling like I had to fight for my place in the world.

As the conversation wound down, Grandma's voice softened. "You'll come visit this summer, right? It'll be good for you to see everyone."

"Yeah, Grandma," I said, my voice a little too flat to sound convincing.

I hung up the phone and stared at it for a moment, the sound of her voice still echoing in my mind. She meant well, I knew that. But the thought of going back, of facing Fortune and Majesty, made my chest tighten. Still, I clung to the promise of safety, however temporary it was. I just wanted to belong. And if I couldn't have that, at least I had Grandma—for the summer, at least.

CHAPTER 8: A DESPERATE NEED TO BE SEEN

The days following my disclosure to Ms. Smith were a confusing mix of relief and anxiety. The secret was out, the burden shared, but the fear of repercussions lingered, a dark cloud hovering over my head. JJ remained a constant threat, his presence a shadow that followed me everywhere, lurking in the corners of my mind even when he wasn't physically near.

At school, I found solace in the familiar routine. Ms. Smith's classroom became my sanctuary, a place where I could momentarily forget the turmoil that plagued my life. I excelled in my studies, my thirst for knowledge a welcome distraction from the darkness that threatened to consume me. With each lesson, each completed assignment, I built a fragile sense of control over my chaotic world.

But my solace was often disrupted by my own actions. I craved attention, connection—any acknowledgment that I existed. Yet, my attempts to connect with the other children often backfired. My words and actions landed with a resounding thud in the chasm between our worlds. They played with an ease I couldn't comprehend, their laughter free of the weight that pressed so heavily on my shoulders.

One afternoon, desperation clawed at me, the need to be noticed suffocating. I stood on the playground, my heart hammering in my chest as I pulled up my shirt, revealing the tiny bumps that had become a source of whispered curiosity among my classmates.

"See?" I declared, my voice trembling with a mixture of defiance and shame. "I'm not stuffing my bra!"

For a moment, silence stretched between us, thick and suffocating. The other children stared, their eyes wide with a mixture of curiosity, confusion, and disgust. My defiance wavered. Shame slithered up my spine, wrapping itself around my throat. I felt my face burn, but I couldn't bring myself to lower my shirt just yet. I needed them to see, to understand, to acknowledge me in some way.

A few kids snickered. Some whispered to each other. Others turned away entirely, unwilling to engage with the spectacle I had made of myself. The weight of their reactions crushed me, pressing down like an unbearable weight.

Ms. Smith must have seen the commotion from across the yard, because moments later, she appeared at my side, placing a firm but gentle hand on my shoulder. "Tess, let's go inside for a moment," she said softly, her voice carrying no judgment, only concern.

I let her guide me back into the building, my legs moving on autopilot. She led me to an empty classroom and pulled up a chair, gesturing for me to sit. I did, unable to meet her eyes, my hands twisting in my lap.

"Tess," she began, her voice calm and steady. "Do you want to tell me what that was about?"

I shrugged, my throat tight. "They kept saying I was stuffing my bra," I muttered. "I just wanted them to stop. I wanted them to believe me."

Ms. Smith sighed, leaning forward slightly. "I understand that must have been frustrating. But there are other ways to handle things like that." She hesitated for a moment before continuing, "Are you feeling okay, Tess? Really okay?"

I didn't know how to answer that. I wanted to say yes, to brush it off, to pretend this was just another harmless mistake. But Ms. Smith had been the only adult who had ever really listened to me, and something about the way she looked at me made my defenses crumble just a little.

"I don't know," I admitted, my voice barely above a whisper.

She nodded, as if she had expected that answer. "You don't have to figure it all out on your own, you know. I'm here, and I want to help."

I swallowed hard, emotions warring inside me. I wanted help, but I didn't even know where to start.

Ms. Smith gave me a moment before she spoke again. "How about this—you don't have to explain everything right now. But if you ever want to talk, I'll listen. No judgment, no expectations. Just a safe place for you to say what's on your mind."

Something about her words settled the chaos inside me just a little. I nodded slowly, not quite trusting my voice to speak.

She offered me a small smile before standing. "Come on. Let's get you some water and take a breath, okay?"

I followed her out of the room, still feeling raw and exposed, but not as alone as before. And for now, maybe that was enough.

CHAPTER 9: CAUGHT AND CONSEQUENCES

The weight of the money in my pocket felt heavier than usual. It wasn't much—just a twenty-dollar bill and a five, the exact amount JJ told me to take. I had followed the rules, just like always. But tonight, something felt different.

I had crept into dad's room, moving slow, careful not to breathe too loudly, not to let the floorboards betray me. The wallet was exactly where it always was, tucked inside the top drawer of the nightstand. My fingers worked quickly, barely shaking now. I had done this so many times before that my body moved on instinct.

But as I slipped the money into my pocket and turned to tiptoe back to my room, I heard it.

The unmistakable shift of the bed.

The soft rustling of sheets.

I froze.

"Tess."

My father's voice. Not groggy. Not confused. Just sharp. Awake. Watching.

I turned slowly, my heart pounding so loudly in my ears that I could barely hear my own breath. He was sitting up in bed, his eyes locked on me.

My mouth opened, but no words came out.

"Tess," he said again, this time slower. His eyes flickered to the nightstand, then back to me. "What are you doing?"

My throat was too dry to answer.

"Come here."

I wanted to run, but I knew better. I stepped forward, my legs weak, my mind scrambling for a lie, any lie.

He held out his hand. "Give it to me."

Tears stung my eyes as I reached into my pocket and pulled out the money. I placed it in his outstretched palm, my fingers trembling.

I didn't know what was worse—the way his jaw clenched, the way his hands tightened around the bills, or the look of sheer disappointment in his eyes.

"Tess," he said, his voice low, controlled, dangerous. "Why are you stealing from me?"

I swallowed hard, my mind racing. I couldn't tell the truth. I couldn't tell him about JJ.

"I was... I was gonna give it to some kids at school," I blurted out.

His eyes narrowed. "What?"

I nodded quickly, gripping the hem of my shirt. "They don't have any money. I just wanted to help them."

The lie felt pathetic the second it left my lips.

My father's nostrils flared. "You mean to tell me you're taking my hard-earned money and giving it away?" His voice rose with every word, his frustration turning into something worse.

I knew what was coming.

And yet, when the first strike of the belt hit my skin, it still sent a shock through my body.

I squeezed my eyes shut, biting my lip so hard I tasted blood. I couldn't cry. If I cried, it would only make it worse.

The belt came down again.

And again.

And again.

Each strike burned, but I didn't make a sound.

By the time he was finished, my body felt like it was on fire. I stood there, trembling, my breath coming in short, shallow bursts.

"Go to bed," he muttered, shaking his head. "And don't ever let me catch you stealing again."

I nodded weakly, turning on shaky legs and stumbling out of the room.

I barely made it to my bed before collapsing onto the mattress, my whole body aching. My skin was raw where the belt had struck, but the pain in my chest was worse.

JJ.

I didn't bring him the money.

I curled up into a ball, trying to convince myself that maybe he wouldn't notice, that maybe he wouldn't care. Maybe he would forget.

But deep down, I knew better.

It was sometime after midnight when I felt it.

The soft shift of my mattress.

The cold press of something sharp against my throat.

My eyes flew open, and all I saw was darkness.

Then, a voice.

Low. Calm. Terrifying.

"You think you can steal and not pay up?"

JJ.

My body locked up, my breath catching in my throat. The blade of the knife pressed a little harder, just enough for me to feel its threat.

"You didn't bring me my money," he murmured.

I wanted to speak, wanted to apologize, wanted to say something, but my throat had closed up.

He let out a soft chuckle, like this was funny to him.

"What am I gonna do with you, Tess?"

The knife traced a slow line along my skin, just enough to send shivers through my body.

I didn't move. Didn't breathe.

"You know what happens when you don't follow the rules?" he whispered.

A tear slipped down my cheek.

He pressed the knife just a little harder, right under my chin, tilting my face up toward his unseen gaze.

"I should kill you right now," he said, almost thoughtful.

My heart slammed against my ribs.

Then, just as suddenly as he had appeared, he pulled the knife away. I gasped, my breath rushing back all at once.

"Don't ever do that again," JJ said, his voice ice-cold.

And then he was gone.

I didn't sleep that night.

I didn't sleep for many nights after that.
I had always known JJ was dangerous.
But tonight, he had made sure I understood.
He wasn't just dangerous.
He was deadly.

CHAPTER 10: A KNOCK AT THE DOOR

The next day, I sat at my desk, pretending to focus on my math worksheet, but my mind was a tangled mess. Every time I tried to solve an equation, my thoughts drifted back to JJ's cold voice, the gleam of the knife, and his words: "I'll kill you, Tess." Even now, just thinking about it made my stomach churn.

Ms. Smith stood at the front of the class, her voice calm but firm as she guided us through the lesson. She had always been perceptive, noticing things about me that other teachers missed. And today, her sharp eyes found mine.

After class, she asked me to stay behind. My heart sank.

When the room cleared, she sat down across from me at one of the desks. Her expression was softer than usual, but her eyes were searching.

"Tess, I've been thinking about what you said the other day," she began, her voice gentle but firm. "About your brother hitting you."

I froze, the memory of JJ's threats surging forward like a wave. My instinct to protect myself—and him—kicked in immediately.

"I was kidding," I said quickly, forcing a nervous laugh. "I didn't mean it."

Ms. Smith didn't smile. She tilted her head, watching me closely. "Kidding about something like that isn't funny, Tess. It's serious. And lying is a sin."

I looked down at my hands, twisting my fingers together under the desk. I knew she didn't believe me, and I could feel her concern like a weight pressing down on my chest. But I couldn't tell her the truth. I couldn't let JJ find out I had talked about him again.

"I'm not lying," I mumbled, my voice barely above a whisper.

"Tess," she said, leaning in slightly. "If something is going on at home, you can tell me. You know that, right? I can help."

I nodded, but I didn't say anything else. The silence stretched between us, heavy and suffocating. Finally, she sighed and stood up.

"All right," she said. "Go on. But remember, lying doesn't help anyone—not you, not your family, and certainly not the people who care about you."

Her words lingered in my mind for the rest of the day. Lying was a sin. But wasn't lying the only thing keeping me safe? If I told the truth, JJ would make good on his threats. I was sure of it.

When I got home, I carried the weight of her words with me, replaying the conversation over and over. I didn't talk much during dinner, avoiding my dad's and stepmother's eyes. Afterward, I sat in my room, staring at the wall, trying to block out the thoughts swirling in my head.

My dad got ready to go out for the night, his cologne filling the apartment as he prepared for another date. He barely said goodbye before he and my stepmother left, the door clicking shut behind them. I was alone with JJ now, but I kept to myself, trying not to draw his attention. Hours passed. The silence of the apartment was broken only by the faint hum of the refrigerator and the occasional creak of the floorboards. I had just started to relax when there was a knock at the door.

I froze.

JJ peeked out of his room, frowning. "Who is that?" he hissed, his voice low.

"I don't know," I whispered back, my heart pounding. He motioned for me to go check, and I hesitated before creeping to the door. When I peeked through the peephole, my breath caught in my throat.

It was a social worker.

CHAPTER 11: THE KNOCK

The knock at the door was loud, echoing through the stillness of the apartment. My chest tightened as I opened the door just enough to peek out. Standing there was a woman with a clipboard, dressed in slacks and a button-up shirt. Her expression was calm but serious, the kind of look that told me she was here for something important.

"Hi, sweetheart," she said softly. "Is your mom or dad home?"

I hesitated, gripping the edge of the door tightly. "No, they're on a date," I said, my voice barely above a whisper.

Her eyes softened, and she crouched slightly, trying to meet my gaze. "Okay. Who's here with you?"

I glanced over my shoulder toward the hallway, where JJ's room was, before looking back at her. "My older brother," I replied.

She nodded, her pen scratching against the clipboard. "Can I ask you something, Tess? Are you safe here? Is anyone hurting you?"

My throat tightened, and for a moment, I thought about telling her everything. The bruises, the welts, the knife, the threats. But JJ's voice echoed in my head: "I'll kill you." The fear of what he might do if I talked kept my lips sealed.

"No," I said quickly. "I'm fine. Nobody's hurting me." Her eyes lingered on me for a moment, as if she could see through the lie. But instead of pressing further, she stood up straight. "Can I speak with your brother?"

I nodded and called for JJ, my voice shaking. He appeared from his room moments later, his expression neutral but his eyes calculating. The social worker introduced herself and started asking questions.

I stepped back into the hallway, watching from a distance as they talked near the front door. JJ's tone was calm and collected, his smile practiced and disarming. He had a way of making himself seem trustworthy, like he could charm his way out of anything. I couldn't hear much of what they were saying, but I caught fragments.

"She's a troubled child," JJ said smoothly, gesturing toward me. "Always looking for attention, you know how kids can be. She's been stealing from Dad, and when she gets in trouble, she tries to blame me for it."

The social worker nodded, jotting something down on her clipboard. I felt my stomach drop as JJ continued spinning his story, making everything sound like it was my fault. I wanted to shout, to tell her he was lying, but the fear kept me rooted in place.

"She's a good kid," JJ added, his voice dripping with fake warmth. "She just gets carried away sometimes. We're doing our best to help her, though."

The social worker gave him a small smile and handed him a card before thanking him for his time. JJ closed the door behind her, his calm demeanor vanishing the moment she was gone. His eyes locked onto mine, cold and furious.

I didn't wait for him to speak. I bolted down the hallway, my feet barely touching the ground as I raced to the bathroom. I slammed the door shut and locked it, my hands trembling as I backed away.

JJ's footsteps were heavy, deliberate, as he walked toward the bathroom. He stopped just outside the door, and the silence that followed was deafening.

CHAPTER 12: THE SILENCE THAT FOLLOWED

The knock on the bathroom door turned into pounding, each hit louder and more forceful. I pressed my back against the door, tears streaming down my face as I screamed, "Go away! Leave me alone!"

"Open the door, Tess!" JJ shouted, his voice filled with anger. "Don't make this worse for yourself!"

I sobbed, my hands trembling as I gripped the edge of the sink for support. "No! I won't let you in!" I cried out, my voice hoarse and desperate.

Then, the banging stopped. Silence filled the air, but it wasn't comforting. It was the kind of silence that made my heart pound harder.

"Tess," a voice said, softer now, but firm. "It's me, Dad. Open the door."

My breath caught. Was it really him? My mind raced. Dad must have come home early. He must have heard everything.

Relief rushed over me as I unlocked the door and cracked it open, ready to run to the safety of my father's arms. But the moment I stepped out, the truth hit me like a freight train. It wasn't Dad.

It was JJ.

I froze, my body paralyzed with fear as I stared at his face, a wicked grin spreading across it. He didn't give me a chance to react. Before I could retreat back into the bathroom, JJ lunged forward, shoving the door wide open and cutting off my escape.

I screamed, but it didn't matter. JJ grabbed my head with both hands, his grip strong and unrelenting. He dragged me toward the kitchen, my feet stumbling beneath me as I fought to break free.

"You think you can embarrass me like that?" he snarled. "You think you can just run to someone else for help?"

I cried and begged, my words jumbled and desperate, but they only seemed to fuel his rage. He slammed my head into the edge of the kitchen sink, the impact sending a sharp, searing pain through my skull. My vision blurred, black spots dancing before my eyes as I crumbled to the floor.

JJ didn't stop. He crouched over me, his fists slamming into my gut, each punch driving the air from my lungs. I tried to curl into myself, to protect my body, but there was no escape. My sobs turned to gasps, and then silence.

When he couldn't get to my stomach, JJ shifted his focus. He stomped his foot into my lower body, hard and fast, targeting my most vulnerable spot. Once. Twice. Three times. Four. Pain erupted through me, radiating from my core as I folded in on myself, powerless to stop him.

After that, everything faded. The world around me dissolved into darkness, and I welcomed the escape, even if it was only temporary.

I woke up in my bed, the room dimly lit by the glow of the hallway light. My body ached in ways I couldn't describe, but there was no sharp pain. No marks or bruises. Nothing visible. It was as if the violence had left no physical evidence, just the silent torment that lingered in its wake.

From the kitchen, I could hear the sound of silverware clinking against plates and the low hum of voices. They were having dinner. JJ's voice cut through the quiet, light and casual, as if nothing had happened.

"She went to bed early," he said, his tone nonchalant. "She wasn't feeling well."

I stayed where I was, curled up under the covers, unwilling to move. The thought of facing JJ—or anyone—felt impossible. My body might not have shown the scars, but inside, I felt broken, shattered into pieces I wasn't sure I'd ever put back together.

I stared at the wall, tears sliding silently down my face. I didn't want to think, I didn't want to feel. I just wanted to disappear.

CHAPTER 13: THE STAIN

The first thing I noticed was the blood in my underwear. My heart sank as I stared down at it, my mind racing with a mix of fear and shame. I didn't cry. I didn't panic. I just stood there in the bathroom, frozen, staring at the undeniable evidence of what had happened.

The bathroom door creaked open, and my stepmom walked in. She had a habit of barging in without knocking, but this time, her timing couldn't have been worse. I was sitting on the toilet, too stunned to react, when she caught sight of the blood. Her eyes widened in shock.

"What... what is this?" she stammered, pointing at the stained underwear. Her voice was sharp, rising in pitch as her panic set in. "Tess, what is this? What happened?"

I couldn't answer. My lips stayed shut as she stepped closer, her movements frantic. Her panic made the moment feel even more unbearable.

She grabbed the edge of the bathroom door and slammed it shut just as my father's footsteps approached. "What's going on in there?" he shouted, his voice muffled through the door.

"Just a minute!" she yelled back, her tone snapping with urgency.

She turned back to me, her face a mixture of anger and desperation. She dropped to her knees in front of me, her hands gripping my shoulders. "Tess," she said, her voice trembling. "What happened? Tell me the truth."

I shook my head, refusing to meet her eyes. She had whooped me plenty of times before, always believing I was a rebellious, disobedient child. But now, for the first time, she looked at me differently. Her voice cracked as she pleaded, her own tears welling up. "Tess, please. What happened? Who did this to you?"

I mumbled, "Nothing."

Her grip on my shoulders tightened. "Nothing? Look at me!" she cried. "There's blood. Someone hurt you. What happened? Tell me!"

I wanted to say it. I wanted to tell her about JJ, about the stomping, about the pain and the fear. But the words wouldn't come. JJ's threats echoed in my mind. "I'll kill you." I couldn't risk it. I couldn't take the chance.

"The girls at school," I blurted out suddenly. "They did it. They were bullying me."

She froze, her mouth slightly open, trying to process my words. "The girls at school?" she repeated, her tone disbelieving. "Are you lying to me, Tess? Don't lie to me!"

I shook my head, tears burning my eyes but refusing to fall. "They did it," I whispered.

She stared at me, her own tears spilling over. There was anger in her voice when she spoke again, but it wasn't directed at me. "Why didn't you tell me? Why would you let this happen?"

The banging on the door came again, harder this time. "What's going on in there?" my dad demanded.

"Just a minute!" she yelled again, her voice sharp. She turned back to me, her face crumpled with worry. "Tess, you have to tell me the truth. I can't help you if you don't tell me the truth."

But I didn't say anything else. I had nothing left to give. I stared at the tiled floor, silent, my body stiff under her gaze.

Later that day, she took me to the doctor. I sat on the cold examination table, my hands folded in my lap, as the doctor examined me. My stepmom stood by the door, her arms crossed, her face a mask of tension.

When the doctor finished, I heard her whisper the question she had been too afraid to ask in front of me. "Is her hymen still intact?"

The doctor nodded, his voice calm but clinical. "Yes, it's intact. There's some scar tissue, but no signs of penetration. It looks like she may have been hit in that area or had a significant impact, like falling on something."

My stepmom's shoulders sagged with relief, but her expression remained grim. She nodded, thanked the doctor, and we left the office in silence.

The car ride home was heavy. The tension filled the air, choking out any possibility of conversation. My stepmom kept glancing at me in the rearview mirror, her eyes flicking back and forth between the road and my face. I avoided her gaze, staring out the window as the scenery blurred past.

She wanted answers. I could feel it in every glance she gave me. But I had none to give. I sat silently, my hands resting in my lap, my face emotionless. No tears. No words. Nothing.

When we got home, I went straight to my room and crawled into bed. I could hear my dad asking my stepmom what was going on, but she didn't answer. The sounds of their voices faded into the background as I pulled the covers over my head, shutting out the world. I stayed there, motionless, my body aching but my face blank. This was my life. This was how it had always been. And deep down, I knew it would never change. Nothing would change. Not until the day I died.

CHAPTER 14 - THE SILENCE BETWEEN THE STORMS

The days following the doctor's visit passed in a haze. I drifted through them like a ghost, feeling disconnected from everything around me. The house had its usual rhythm—my father working, Barbara cooking, JJ watching from the corners of rooms like a shadow that never left. But inside me, something had shifted.

I had never truly believed in being saved. Even as Barbara's panic had overtaken her in the bathroom, even when she had taken me to the doctor, I had known deep down that nothing would change.

And I had been right.

Barbara hadn't brought up the incident again. Maybe she wanted to believe my lie about the girls at school, or maybe she had simply decided that since the doctor hadn't confirmed her worst fear, it was easier to move forward in silence. Either way, she let it go.

My father never even asked. He had learned to trust Barbara's judgment, to let her handle things, and she had handled this by doing nothing at all.

I sat in my room, staring at the ceiling, wondering if anyone in this house actually saw me.

At dinner that night, I barely touched my food. The voices of my father and Barbara hummed around me, mixing with the clinking of silverware against plates. JJ sat across from me, eating like nothing had happened. Like he hadn't crushed me under his heel, like he hadn't left scars on my skin and deeper ones inside of me.

"Eat your food, Tess," Barbara said, nudging my plate toward me.

I picked up my fork and took a small bite, forcing myself to chew.

"JJ, did you finish your homework?" my father asked.

JJ nodded. "Yeah, I did it earlier."

He was lying. I knew it, Barbara probably knew it, but my father just nodded and moved on.

JJ glanced at me, a slow smirk curling on his lips.

I dropped my gaze, suddenly feeling sick to my stomach.

That night, I lay in bed, the house quiet except for the occasional creak of the walls settling. I had grown used to sleeping lightly, always waiting, always anticipating the next thing that would go wrong.

The door to my room creaked open. My breath hitched, my body going rigid under the blankets.

JJ's footsteps were soft against the carpet as he walked over to my bed. He crouched down beside me, his voice barely above a whisper.

"No one's coming to save you," he murmured.

I didn't move. Didn't breathe.

"No one believes you," he continued, his breath hot against my ear. "Not Dad. Not Barbara. Not even your precious teachers."

I squeezed my eyes shut.

"Now, be good, or next time…" He let the words hang in the air before standing up and walking back to the door.

The silence he left behind was deafening.

I didn't sleep that night.

The next morning, Barbara acted like nothing had happened. She packed lunches, kissed my father goodbye as he left for work, and reminded me and JJ to behave. I watched her, searching her face for something—anything—that would tell me she still had questions, that she still cared.

But there was nothing.
And for the first time, I truly understood.
I was alone.
I swallowed hard, grabbed my backpack, and headed toward the door. I wasn't ready for school, wasn't ready to see anyone, but at least there, I could be someone else.
At least there, I could pretend.

CHAPTER 15: THE BURNING LESSON

The weekend came around, and as usual, errands filled the day. The three of us—Barbara, JJ, and I—piled into the old 2000s Honda. Barbara was in charge of groceries for dinner, and we stopped at the local store to grab what we needed. She parked the car, told us to stay put, and headed inside with her purse slung over her shoulder.

The car fell silent as the trunk door slammed shut behind her.

I sat in the back seat, staring out the window, counting the cracks in the pavement to distract myself from the oppressive stillness. JJ was in the front seat, leaning back comfortably, his eyes focused on something in the dashboard.

I didn't realize what he was doing until I saw the faint glow of orange in his hand. The car lighter. One of those old ones that heated up in the center console, meant for lighting cigarettes. He pressed it in, and I watched as it clicked, the faint hiss of heat filling the silence.

I looked away, hoping to avoid his attention, but his voice broke the quiet.

"Tess," he said, his tone light and casual, like he was starting a friendly conversation. But there was something behind it, something that made my stomach twist.

I didn't answer right away, hoping he'd lose interest. But when I glanced up, he had turned around in his seat, his eyes fixed on me with a smile that didn't reach them.

"Tess," he said again, his voice lower now, more deliberate. "Have you ever wondered what it would feel like to burn?"

My heart stopped for a moment. "No," I said quickly, shaking my head.

He tilted his head, studying me like I was some sort of experiment. Then he smiled again. "I think you have. Don't lie to me."

"I haven't," I said, my voice trembling.

He reached back, grabbed my arm, and yanked it toward him. "Let's find out," he said, his voice calm and measured, like he was discussing the weather.

I tried to pull away, panic surging through me. "No! No, JJ, stop!" I cried, my voice cracking. But my pleas only seemed to amuse him.

"Shut it," he said sharply, his smile never faltering. He held my arm firmly, positioning it just right. Then, before I could react, he grabbed the glowing car lighter and stamped it onto my skin.

The pain was immediate and excruciating. My body jolted, and I opened my mouth to scream, but no sound came out. His grip on my arm tightened as I thrashed, my silent screams locked behind my clenched teeth.

"Don't cry," he hissed, his voice low and threatening. "If you cry, I'll do it again."

I bit down on my lip so hard I tasted blood, my tears burning as they slid down my cheeks. The smell of burnt skin filled the car, and I felt like I was going to pass out. He finally pulled the lighter away, inspecting the mark he'd left on my arm with a satisfied smirk.

"Wipe your face," he said coldly. "And shut up before you get more."

I wiped at my cheeks with trembling hands, trying to erase any sign of what had just happened. My entire arm throbbed, the pain radiating through my body, but I forced myself to stay quiet. I should have known he stopped for a reason.

Out of the corner of my eye, I saw Barbara pushing the grocery cart back toward the car. JJ must have seen her too, because he turned around in his seat and leaned back, as if nothing had happened.

The trunk opened with a soft creak as Barbara began loading the bags. My hands fumbled to tuck my arm into my lap, hiding the angry red mark beneath the folds of my shirt. I had less than two minutes to compose myself, to wipe my tears, to make it look like nothing had happened.

Barbara came around to the driver's seat, opened the door, and slid in. I squeezed my eyes shut, pretending to be asleep as she adjusted the mirror and started the car.

"You two okay?" she asked, her tone casual.

"Yeah," JJ said smoothly. "She fell asleep while you were gone. She's fine."

Barbara glanced in the rearview mirror, and for a moment, I thought she might say something. But she didn't. She put the car in reverse, and we drove off, the weight of what had just happened hanging heavy in the air.

I kept my eyes shut the entire ride home, my body tense, my arm throbbing. I didn't need to open them to know JJ was staring at me, a smug smile on his face. I didn't need to hear him say it to know what he was thinking.

He really is going to kill me.

CHAPTER 16: FRAGILE PEACE

Sunday began like most Sundays. Barbara was up early, moving around the house in her housecoat, humming to herself as she planned dinner. The smell of freshly brewed coffee wafted from the kitchen, mixing with the faint scent of furniture polish from her morning cleaning routine. The air felt lighter today, almost as if the house itself had decided to take a break from the usual tension.

I lingered in my room, slowly getting out of bed. My body still ached from the week before, but I pushed the feeling aside. Sunday was different—quieter, slower. I dressed carefully, knowing Barbara wouldn't tolerate me looking disheveled, even if we weren't going anywhere. The small sounds of normalcy—the clink of a coffee cup being set down, the faint hum of the radio in the kitchen—were oddly comforting.

JJ was already up, sitting on the couch with a bowl of cereal balanced on his lap. He barely looked up as I walked past him to the kitchen. Dad was there, leaning against the counter with his coffee in hand, his eyes still heavy with sleep. Barbara glanced at me as I came in. "Good morning," she said, her tone neutral but polite. "Tess, take the trash out before you do anything else." I nodded, grabbing the overflowing bag by the door. The morning air was cool and crisp, the faint sound of birds chirping in the distance. For a moment, I stood outside, breathing in the quiet. It was a small reprieve before returning to the house.

By mid-morning, Barbara had already begun cooking dinner. The kitchen smelled amazing—garlic, onions, and herbs sizzling in a pan. She had every burner on the stove going, pots bubbling and pans searing. She barked orders to JJ and me, telling us to help where we could. I peeled potatoes while JJ reluctantly chopped carrots, grumbling under his breath the entire time.

"Stop complaining," Barbara snapped, not looking up from the chicken she was seasoning. "You're old enough to help around here."

JJ rolled his eyes, but he kept chopping. I stayed quiet, focusing on my task and hoping to avoid any attention.

The last thing I wanted was for the fragile peace of the day to shatter.

Around noon, Dad decided to head to the hardware store. He wasn't much for staying idle on Sundays, always finding an excuse to tinker with something around the house. JJ tried to tag along, but Barbara stopped him.

"You've got homework to finish," she said firmly. "Stay here and help Tess with hers too."

JJ groaned but didn't argue. Once Dad left, the house felt quieter, the TV droning in the background as Barbara continued her cooking. JJ plopped down at the kitchen table, pulling my math workbook toward him.

"Let's just get this over with," he said, flipping through the pages.

I sat beside him, surprised by his sudden willingness to help. He worked through a few problems with me, explaining them in a way that was almost patient. Almost. When I got something wrong, his tone would sharpen, but for the most part, he kept his temper in check. For a moment, he almost seemed like a real big brother.

By the time dinner was ready, the house was filled with the rich smells of roasted chicken, buttery mashed potatoes, and steamed vegetables. Barbara called everyone to the table, and we all sat down together. The conversation was light, mostly about plans for the week ahead. Barbara told Dad about the Johnsons inviting us over for dinner next weekend.

"I told them we'd come," she said, pouring herself a glass of water. "They've been asking us for weeks."

"Sounds good," Dad said, nodding. "It'll be nice to get out of the house."

I picked at my food, feeling a knot of unease at the mention of the Johnsons. I didn't know them well, but I wasn't eager to go. Still, I kept quiet, hoping no one would notice.

After dinner, Barbara insisted that JJ and I help clean up. JJ washed dishes while I dried them, both of us working in silence. Dad sat in the living room, flipping through channels, the low murmur of the TV filling the background. Once the kitchen was spotless, Barbara announced she was going to take a bath and disappeared down the hallway.

The three of us—Dad, JJ, and I—ended up in the living room, watching an old sitcom. For a moment, it felt normal. JJ laughed at the jokes, leaning back on the couch with his feet propped up on the coffee table. Dad chuckled too, his arm slung lazily over the back of the couch.

As the evening wore on, Dad suggested we play pool on the computer, something we did often. JJ and I took turns with him, the clacking sound of virtual balls filling the room. JJ hated waiting for his turn, grumbling every time he had to pass the mouse. But Dad kept the mood light, teasing him when he missed a shot and laughing when I somehow managed to sink one by accident.

For the first time in what felt like forever, the evening ended peacefully. JJ didn't lose his temper, Barbara didn't snap, and Dad seemed genuinely relaxed. I crawled into bed that night with a strange feeling—a flicker of hope that maybe, just maybe, tomorrow could be normal too.

But deep down, I knew better. Peace never lasted long in our house.

CHAPTER 17: THE WEIGHT OF EXPECTATIONS

The week passed in a strange blur, each day feeling heavier than the last. The routine was the same—school, home, dinner, homework—but underneath the surface, tension simmered, like an ever-present storm cloud threatening to break.

Early in the week, I stole from Dad again. This time, I made sure it was enough money to satisfy JJ. I'd learned my lesson. I followed his rules to the letter, carefully counting the bills in Dad's wallet and taking only what JJ had instructed. My hands trembled as I slipped the money out, but the anxiety wasn't as sharp as it had been before. I was starting to get used to it, and that realization scared me more than anything.

When I handed JJ the money, he took it without a word. He didn't berate me or make any threats. Instead, he pocketed the cash and walked away, leaving me standing there in the hallway. No beatings. No bruises. For once, I was able to breathe.

But the relief was fleeting. At school, I couldn't seem to keep myself in check. I interrupted the teacher, talked over my classmates, and found every excuse to draw attention to myself. I didn't know why I did it. Maybe I was testing boundaries, searching for control in a life where I had none. Maybe I just wanted someone to see me—to really see me—and understand that something was wrong.

By midweek, my teacher, Ms. Smith, had reached her limit. "Tess," she said sharply during math, her patience clearly worn thin. "Come to the front of the class."

I hesitated, my heart sinking as I stood and shuffled to the front of the room. She handed me two heavy books, her expression stern. "Hold these out," she instructed, motioning for me to stretch my arms forward.

I obeyed, the weight of the books quickly pulling at my shoulders. "I'm sorry," I whispered, but Ms. Smith wasn't swayed.

"You'll stay like that until you learn how to behave," she said firmly.

The classroom was silent, all eyes on me as I stood there, arms trembling under the weight of the books. Tears pricked at my eyes, and soon they spilled over, hot and fast. My nose ran, snot bubbling as I tried to hold back my sobs. The humiliation was unbearable, but I didn't dare complain. I just stood there, enduring it.

When Ms. Smith finally let me sit down, I kept my head down for the rest of the day, the heat of embarrassment still burning in my cheeks. The rest of the week, I was on my best behavior—not out of guilt, but out of fear. I didn't want to be singled out again, to feel the weight of everyone's eyes on me.

Friday came, marking the end of the school year. There was a buzz of excitement in the air as students cleaned out their desks and hugged their friends goodbye. But I felt none of that excitement. I walked home with my report card clutched in my hand, my stomach twisting with both pride and dread.

When I got home, I handed the report card to Dad, standing silently as he read through the comments. His face softened when he saw the grades—straight A's, as I'd expected—but his expression darkened when he reached the behavior section.

"Tess," he said, shaking his head, "what's this?"

I bit my lip as he read the comments aloud. Talks a lot in class. Doesn't get along with peers. Struggles with group assignments. Each one felt like a slap, even though I already knew what they said.

"You can't act like this in school," he said firmly, his disappointment clear. "You're too smart for this nonsense."

I nodded, swallowing the lump in my throat. But then his tone shifted, and a small smile broke through his stern expression. "Straight A's, though," he said, his pride showing. "That's something."

He rewarded me for my academic grades, handing me a few dollars and ruffling my hair. I wanted to feel happy, to bask in the small victory, but the praise felt hollow. I couldn't shake the feeling that my behavior would always overshadow my accomplishments.

JJ's report card came home the same day. He tried to avoid handing it over, but Dad wasn't having it. "Let me see it," Dad said, holding out his hand.

JJ reluctantly placed the paper in Dad's hand, his jaw tight, his shoulders tense. I stood in the corner, holding my breath, waiting for the inevitable explosion.

The silence that followed was thick and heavy. Dad's face darkened as he scanned the report card, his lips pressing into a thin line.

"Ds and Fs," Dad finally said, his voice low and full of disappointment. He shook the paper in front of JJ. "This? This is what you've been doing in school?"

JJ didn't say anything, his eyes fixed on the floor.

"You're failing," Dad continued, his voice rising. "You're a failure. Is that what you want to be? A failure?"

I flinched at the word, the sharpness of it cutting through the air. JJ's fists clenched at his sides, his face turning red, but he didn't speak. He just stood there, his jaw tight, as Dad berated him, going on and on about how he needed to do better, how he wasn't trying hard enough.

I couldn't tell if Dad was trying to motivate him or just venting his frustration, but either way, the words clearly stung. JJ's eyes flicked toward me for a brief moment, and the anger in his gaze made my stomach drop.

I hated this. I hated the way the attention shifted from my behavior to his grades, as if the spotlight of disappointment was something that could be passed around. I hated the way JJ looked at me, like it was my fault he was being called a failure. I hated the guilt that settled in my chest, even though I hadn't done anything wrong.

That night, as I lay in bed, I couldn't stop replaying the scene in my head. The tension at home always found a way to creep into every corner of my life, even when I wasn't the one in trouble. JJ's angry eyes were the last thing I saw before I fell asleep, a reminder that peace in our house was always temporary.

CHAPTER 18: SHADOWS ON THE WALL

Barbara's friends' house was bustling with activity. Laughter and conversation floated through the air, the parents huddled together in the living room as they caught up over snacks and drinks. The house was big, with worn carpets that carried the faint smell of old furniture and years of lived-in memories.

Barbara's friend greeted us warmly, ushering us inside and motioning toward the upstairs where the kids were. "The boys are up there," she said with a smile. "Go join them."

I followed JJ up the creaky staircase, trailing behind him like a shadow. My stomach churned with unease, though I couldn't pinpoint why. Upstairs, Dominic was sitting cross-legged on the floor, a PlayStation controller in his hand as he focused on the screen. The room was dim, lit only by the glow of the TV and a small lamp in the corner.

"Hey," Dominic said without looking away from the game. JJ gave him a nod before sitting down beside him, the two of them immediately engrossed in whatever was on the screen. I stood awkwardly near the doorway, unsure of where to go or what to do.

After a while, I grabbed a blanket from the corner of the couch and curled up under it. I felt invisible, like I wasn't really there. The hum of the video game, the occasional burst of laughter from the living room downstairs—it all blurred together as I lay under the blanket, staring into nothingness. I wasn't part of their world, just a presence in the room.

Out of nowhere, Dominic's voice broke through the silence. "I'm horny," he said, his tone casual, like he was commenting on the weather.

I froze under the blanket, my heart pounding in my chest. My body tensed, every muscle on high alert as his words hung in the air.

JJ glanced at Dominic, then turned to me. "Tess, come here," he said, his voice low and commanding.

I didn't move at first. I didn't want to. Every instinct in my body screamed at me to stay where I was, to stay hidden under the blanket. But JJ's tone left no room for argument. Slowly, I crawled out from under the blanket, my movements hesitant, my stomach twisting with dread.

Dominic grabbed my arm and pulled me toward him. Before I could react, he yanked down my pants and underwear in one swift motion, leaving me exposed. "Get on all fours," he said, his voice steady, almost detached.

I obeyed, my body moving as if on autopilot. My knees pressed into the rough carpet, my hands trembling as I braced myself on the floor. JJ stood in the hallway, leaning against the doorframe, his eyes fixed on the staircase. He was the lookout, making sure no parents came upstairs.

Dominic positioned himself behind me, his hands rough and unkind as he tried to force himself inside. The sharp burn of pain spread through my body as he pressed against me, the rim of my butt stinging with each attempt. I bit my lip to keep from crying out, my hands clutching the carpet as I tried to endure it.

He pushed harder, grunting in frustration as he struggled to fit. The pain was unbearable, a searing heat that made my whole body tense. I wanted to scream, to cry, but I stayed silent. JJ's presence in the hallway was a constant reminder that I couldn't make a sound.

After what felt like an eternity, Dominic stopped. He couldn't get in, couldn't force himself further. The burning pain faded slowly, leaving behind only a dull ache. He sighed in frustration and pulled away, leaving me crumpled on the floor.

Without a word, he picked up the PlayStation controller and resumed the game, as if nothing had happened. JJ stayed in the hallway for a moment longer, his eyes scanning the staircase, before stepping back into the room. He didn't look at me, didn't acknowledge what had just taken place. To him, it was nothing.

Discarded, I reached for my underwear and pants, pulling them up with shaky hands. My movements were mechanical, my mind numb. I crawled back under the blanket, curling into myself as I stared at the ceiling.

I didn't cry. I didn't think. I just lay there, my mind blank, my body heavy with exhaustion. The muffled sounds of the game filled the room, Dominic and JJ laughing occasionally, as if everything was perfectly normal.

I stared at the ceiling, my thoughts distant and detached. I wasn't thinking about anything in particular—just the shapes and shadows that danced on the walls as the glow from the TV flickered. I was nothing in that moment, a shell of myself, existing but not truly living.

CHAPTER 19: THE WEIGHT OF SILENCE

The night after leaving Barbara's friend's house, I lay in bed, staring at the ceiling. The blankets felt heavy, like they were trying to suffocate me. The walls of my room seemed to close in tighter with every breath I took. I hadn't cried. Not then. Not after.

Dominic and JJ had gone back to their video game as if nothing had happened. As if I hadn't been there, on all fours, humiliated and discarded.

I curled deeper under the covers, my knees pressed against my chest. The house was quiet now. Too quiet. My father and Barbara were still downstairs, probably watching TV, lost in whatever sitcom was on that night. The laughter from the show would drift up the stairs occasionally, so wildly out of place in my world that it felt like a cruel joke.

JJ had gone to his room without a word. That, more than anything, made my stomach turn. Usually, he taunted me, whispered threats into the dark, made sure I knew who was in control. But tonight, there was nothing.

I should've been grateful. Instead, I felt a different kind of fear settle in. The waiting was the worst part.

I squeezed my eyes shut, trying to block out the memory.

I thought about Grandma. About her pancakes, the way the syrup dripped slowly down the sides. About the way her house smelled—like old wood and lavender.

One more week.

I repeated it like a mantra.

One more week, and I would be there.

One more week, and I wouldn't have to look at JJ.

One more week, and I could let my body heal without worrying about the next wound.

But a week felt like an eternity.

The next morning, I moved through the house in a fog. Barbara cooked breakfast, humming softly as she flipped eggs in the pan. The smell of butter and toast filled the kitchen, but it made my stomach churn.

JJ sat at the table, shoveling food into his mouth like nothing had happened. Like we hadn't been in that room last night. Like he hadn't stood guard while Dominic tried to—

I forced the thought away, gripping my fork tighter.

"Eat your food, Tess," Barbara said, her voice light but firm. "You barely touched dinner last night."

I nodded and took a small bite of my eggs, forcing myself to chew. It tasted like nothing.

Dad sat at the head of the table, flipping through the newspaper. It was one of the few constants in our home—the way he buried himself in newsprint, ignoring the world around him. I wondered if he ever really looked at me, if he ever really saw me.

The conversation was dull, just talk about errands and things that needed fixing around the house. JJ chimed in occasionally, playing the role of the dutiful son.

JJ nudged my foot under the table.

I flinched.

His smirk was barely noticeable, just a slight curl of his lips as he reached for his orange juice.

Barbara didn't notice.

Dad didn't notice.

No one ever noticed.

Chapter 20: The Playground Confession

The next morning, the weight of my secret felt heavier than my backpack. My stomach churned as I walked into the school, the fluorescent lights in the hallway making everything feel unreal—like I was floating through a dream I couldn't wake up from.

The morning dragged on in a blur of lessons I wasn't paying attention to. The words on the board might as well have been written in another language. I could hear my teacher's voice, but none of it stuck. My mind kept replaying the night before, like a broken record.

I wasn't sure why, but I felt like I had to tell someone. Maybe if I said it out loud, it would make sense. Maybe I wouldn't feel so alone.

By the time recess came, I felt like I was going to burst. The playground was loud with the sounds of kids yelling, playing tag, and swinging on the monkey bars. I walked around aimlessly, my arms wrapped around myself, feeling like I was outside of everything.

Then I saw her. She wasn't exactly my friend, but she was someone I talked to sometimes. Someone I knew well enough to blurt something out to without thinking too hard about it.

I walked right up to her.

"I'm pregnant."

The words came out before I could stop them. It wasn't planned. It wasn't something I thought through. It just spilled from my lips like a secret too heavy to hold.

Her eyes widened. She blinked, processing what I had just said. I could see the way her mind raced, trying to figure out if I was serious or if this was some kind of weird joke.

She didn't ask me anything. She didn't laugh.

Instead, she turned on her heel and marched straight toward the recess monitor—a staff member who stood near the fence, watching over the playground like a hawk.

My stomach dropped.

I stood frozen in place, watching as my classmate whispered something to the staff member, occasionally glancing back at me. My hands felt clammy. My face burned.

The recess monitor furrowed her brow and waved me over.

I walked slowly, my feet heavy, feeling the stares of other kids around me.

She looked down at me, her arms crossed. "Sweetheart, that's not something to joke about," she said, her tone firm but not exactly harsh.

I swallowed hard. "I'm not joking."

She gave me a look—one of those looks adults give when they think they know better than you. The kind that says, *Okay, let's not make things up now.*

"You need to stop saying things like that," she said, shaking her head. "Go play."

I nodded, even though I wanted to scream.

She didn't believe me.

She didn't even consider that I might be telling the truth.

I walked away, feeling numb. I could hear kids laughing nearby, the sound of sneakers scuffing against the pavement, the squeak of the swings. The world kept moving like nothing had happened.

I went through the rest of the school day like a ghost.

At lunch, I sat at the table, picking at my food, hearing the buzz of conversations around me but not really listening. My appetite was gone. I had spoken my truth, and it had been dismissed like it was nothing.

In the classroom, I barely lifted my pencil. The teacher called on me once, but I had no idea what the question was. She sighed and moved on.

By the time the final bell rang, I felt like I had lived a whole lifetime in a single day.

As I walked home, my hands stuffed into my pockets, I realized something—

No one believed me.

And I didn't know if anyone ever would.

CHAPTER 21: ONE MORE WEEK

The phone rang, breaking the stillness of the late afternoon. Barbara handed it to me without a word, already knowing who it was. "It's your grandma," she said, her tone distracted as she busied herself with the dishes.

"Hi, Grandma," I said softly into the receiver, my voice a mix of nerves and relief.

"Hi, Teresa," she replied, her voice warm but firm, the name landing like a pebble thrown into still water. I hated that name. Every time she said it, it felt like a reminder of how little control I had over my life. I couldn't choose where I lived, who I lived with, or even my own name.

But if that was the worst thing I had to deal with today, so be it. I wasn't about to let something as small as a name bother me when my life was filled with bigger battles. "Hi, Grandma," I said again, brushing it off.

"I've been putting my money together for gas," she said. "I'm coming to get you in a week. You'll be here for the summer."

A small flicker of relief passed through me. Summer at Grandma's house was the closest thing I had to a reprieve. Even though I was often picked on by my siblings there, at least I wouldn't be stuck at home with JJ. But that relief was short-lived as I mentally calculated the time. A week. Seven days. I would have to survive another week with him before she came.

"Okay," I said, forcing myself to sound cheerful. "I can't wait."

"Me neither, Teresa," she said. The name stung again, but I let it go. What was the point in correcting her? She'd been calling me that since I was born, and no matter how much I tried to distance myself from it, she wouldn't stop.

"How's school been?" she asked. "Are you still doing well?"

I launched into an account of my report card, telling her about my straight A's and how proud my dad was of my grades—at least academically. I didn't mention the comments about my behavior. I didn't tell her about how Ms. Smith had made me stand at the front of the class with heavy books in my hands as punishment, or how the other kids whispered about me when they thought I couldn't hear. Some things were better left unsaid.

"I like math the most," I told her. "I'm good at it. Really good. My teacher says I'm smart."

"That's wonderful, baby," she said, her voice filled with pride. "You've always been smart."

I smiled faintly, savoring the rare moment of validation. I told her about the school play I had just been in. "I was the only five-year-old in the play because I'm the only one in the elementary school who can read fluently," I said, my chest swelling slightly with pride. "The teacher picked me because I could remember all the lines."

"That's amazing, Teresa," she said, her excitement genuine. "You're doing so well. I'm proud of you."

Her words warmed me, even as the name dug in like a thorn I couldn't pull out. I missed her. I missed the way she cared, the way she listened. She didn't see me as a problem to be solved or a burden to be carried. She saw me.

"I miss you," I said softly.

"I miss you too, baby," she replied. "But I'll see you soon. Just one more week, and you'll be here with me."

We talked for a little while longer, about my siblings, about what she was cooking for dinner that night, about the plans she had for us over the summer. She told me she'd make my favorite breakfast when I got there—pancakes with syrup and sausage on the side. When we finally hung up, I sat there holding the receiver for a moment, letting her words echo in my mind. Just one more week. I could make it through one more week. I had to.

I put the phone back on the hook and went back to my room. For the first time in a long time, I let myself feel the smallest bit of hope. Summer was coming, and with it, a chance to escape—if only for a little while.

Later that day, I tried to keep to myself. I read in my room, letting the words blur together, anything to escape my reality.

JJ stayed out of my way for the most part. That was another red flag.

By the time the sun set, I had convinced myself that maybe—just maybe—he was done. Maybe, for once, I could have peace.

I was wrong.

I woke up to the weight of a body on my chest.

My eyes snapped open, panic gripping me as JJ's face hovered above mine.

His hand clamped over my mouth before I could scream.

"Shhh," he whispered, his breath hot against my cheek.

"You wouldn't want to wake Dad and Barbara, would you?"

I struggled beneath him, but he was stronger.

His knee pressed into my stomach, making it hard to breathe.

"I should kill you," he murmured, almost thoughtful.

I froze.

"I should, you know?" He reached into his pocket and pulled out something cold, pressing it against my throat. The familiar chill of a knife.

Tears welled in my eyes, but I forced them back. He hated when I cried. It only made him worse.

"You think you can go to Grandma's and forget about me?" he whispered, dragging the blade lightly across my skin. "You think she's gonna save you?"

He pressed the knife a little harder.

The sharp edge bit into my flesh, not enough to draw blood but enough to remind me he could.

I didn't move.

I didn't breathe.

"If you ever tell anyone," JJ said, his voice softer now, almost a whisper, "I'll make sure you don't make it to Grandma's."

I believed him.

He lingered a moment longer, letting the weight of his words settle in. Then, just as quickly as he had come, he was gone, slipping out of my room like a shadow.

I stared at the ceiling, my body trembling.

I didn't sleep for the rest of the night.

CHAPTER 22: FRAGILE PEACE

Monday came, and with it, the familiar rhythm of the house waking up. The parents left early for work, their voices muffled as they exchanged last-minute reminders in the kitchen before heading out the door. The sound of the front door shutting was the cue that we were alone for the day—me and JJ.

To my surprise, JJ was in a good mood that morning. He was already in the kitchen when I wandered in, the faint smell of eggs and toast filling the air. "Sit down," he said, motioning to the table with a spatula in hand. "I'm making breakfast."

I hesitated, unsure of what to make of his pleasant demeanor, but I sat anyway. The eggs weren't perfect—scrambled too hard and slightly burnt around the edges—but they were warm and filling. JJ plopped down across from me with his own plate, grinning.

"Let's see who can eat the fastest," he said, picking up his fork. "Ready? Go!"

I didn't want to play, but the way he stared at me, waiting, made it clear I didn't have a choice. I picked up my fork and shoveled eggs into my mouth, chewing as fast as I could. JJ laughed, his mouth full as he finished first, raising his hands in mock victory.

"You're too slow, Tess," he teased. "Better luck next time."

I forced a small smile, grateful that his teasing wasn't cruel this time. For once, the morning felt almost normal. Almost.

Around mid-morning, JJ's friends came over. I heard them before I saw them—the sound of the door creaking open, followed by loud, boisterous voices and the thud of sneakers on the floor. JJ wasn't supposed to have friends over when the parents weren't home, but who was going to tell? Certainly not me.

They crowded into the living room, a group of teenage boys who seemed larger-than-life compared to my small frame. They brought their energy with them, filling the house with laughter and noise. I sat on the floor by the TV, pretending to be engrossed in a cartoon, but I couldn't help listening to their banter.

They told "yo mama" jokes, each one louder and more ridiculous than the last.

"Yo mama so dumb, she tried to climb Mountain Dew!" one of them said, doubling over with laughter.

Another added, "Yo mama so ugly, when she walked by the bathroom, the toilet flushed itself!"

They erupted into laughter, hitting each other's arms and falling over on the couch. JJ joined in, his laugh loud and genuine. It was the kind of laughter that filled the room, making it feel brighter, warmer. For a moment, I wanted to join in too, to be a part of the jokes and the fun. But I stayed where I was, watching from the sidelines.

The house cleared out just before our parents were due home. JJ's friends left as quickly as they had come, their laughter still echoing in the empty living room. JJ stood by the door, waving them off with a grin, before turning back to me.

"Alright," he said, stretching his arms over his head. "Let's eat."

Lunch was simple—peanut butter and jelly sandwiches slapped together in a hurry. We ate on the couch, watching old movies on the TV. JJ picked the movie—a martial arts flick with dramatic fight scenes and over-the-top stunts. He laughed at the ridiculousness of it, while I sat quietly, chewing my sandwich and enjoying the rare calm.

But the calm didn't last. As the afternoon wore on, JJ turned to me, his grin fading. "You know what you have to do before Dad gets home," he said, his tone losing its earlier warmth.

I nodded. JJ had a way of passing off his chores to me, but I didn't argue. It was easier to just do them than to deal with the consequences of saying no. I washed the dishes, the warm water stinging my hands as I scrubbed plates and cups. Then I took out the trash, dragging the heavy bag down the driveway and tossing it into the bin. It wasn't so bad, though. As far as JJ's demands went, this was manageable. By the time Dad's car pulled into the driveway, the house was spotless, and JJ was sitting on the couch, flipping through channels like he hadn't moved all day.

When Dad walked through the door, the familiar heaviness returned to the air. He glanced around the house, nodding in approval at the clean floors and the smell of dinner cooking on the stove. He didn't ask about our day, and we didn't offer any details.

JJ shot me a quick look, a subtle reminder to keep quiet about his friends being over. I didn't need the reminder. I kept my mouth shut, as always, letting the silence settle over the evening.

For all its moments of normalcy, the day ended the way most days did—with an unspoken tension that lingered long after the lights were turned off.

CHAPTER 23: THE PRICE OF PEACE

Tuesday morning started off quiet. JJ was already in the kitchen when I got up, leaning against the counter with a bowl of cereal in one hand and the milk carton in the other. He glanced at me as I walked in, a mischievous smile spreading across his face.

"You want cereal?" he asked, his tone unusually light.

I nodded. "Yeah."

He grabbed another bowl from the cabinet, poured in the cereal, and then added the milk. For a moment, it felt normal—just a big brother making breakfast for his little sister. He slid the bowl across the counter to me, but as I sat down and picked up my spoon, he leaned in close.

"Careful," he said, his voice low. "I think I saw a bug in your food."

I froze, staring down at the cereal. My stomach twisted as I searched the bowl, my appetite disappearing. I hated bugs, and JJ knew it. His grin widened as he watched me, his eyes sparkling with amusement.

"There's no bug," he said after a moment, laughing. "You're so gullible, Tess."

I frowned but didn't say anything. Instead, I quietly ate my cereal, keeping my head down while JJ chuckled to himself. It was his way of keeping me on edge, always unsure whether he was joking or serious.

The rest of the morning passed slowly. JJ lounged around, flipping through channels on the TV while I played quietly with my dolls. Around midday, he suggested we play Barbies together. The idea surprised me—he usually didn't want anything to do with my toys—but I didn't question it.

I grabbed my small collection of dolls from my room and brought them to the living room, where JJ was waiting. He grabbed one of the dolls and started creating a ridiculous storyline, making the Barbie jump off the couch in slow motion as he narrated in an overly dramatic voice. "And then... she FLEW through the air!" he said, tossing the doll into the air before letting it land on the carpet with a soft thud.

I couldn't help but laugh, his antics making the moment feel light and carefree. For a little while, it was just us, goofing off like normal siblings. We created silly voices for the dolls, turning them into spies and superheroes, and laughed until our stomachs hurt. It felt good to laugh, to forget everything else for a little while.

Two days of normalcy in a row. It was almost too good to be true.

That night, as the house settled into its usual quiet, I knew what was coming. JJ cornered me after dinner, his tone sharp and to the point. "Dad's wallet," he said simply. "You know what to do."

I nodded, swallowing the lump in my throat. There was no room to argue, no point in asking why. This was how things were, and I had learned better than to resist.

When the house fell silent, I made my move. I tiptoed into Dad's room, careful not to make a sound. The drawer of his nightstand slid open with a soft creak, and my heart pounded as I carefully counted the bills inside. There were two $20s and a handful of smaller bills. I followed JJ's rules, taking just enough to go unnoticed but enough to satisfy him.

My hands shook as I slipped the money into my pocket and quietly closed the drawer. My escape back to my room was quick and silent, and for the rest of the night, I lay awake, staring at the ceiling and waiting for the other shoe to drop.

Wednesday morning, the shoe dropped. Dad noticed the missing money.

His voice boomed through the house as he demanded answers, his frustration filling every corner of the room. "Who took it?" he asked, his eyes scanning both of us. "Who's stealing from me?"

JJ stayed quiet, his expression calm and detached. I knew he wouldn't admit anything. This was my burden to bear, as it always was.

"It was me," I said, my voice small but steady.

Dad turned to me, his face a mixture of anger and disappointment. "What are you doing with my money, Tess?" he demanded. "Why are you stealing from me?"

I scrambled for an excuse, my mind racing. "I'm giving it to the kids down the street," I blurted out. "They don't have anything, and I wanted to help them."

The lie tumbled out before I could stop it. It wasn't believable—not really—but Dad didn't question it. He sighed deeply, shaking his head. "You don't take money from me, Tess. Ever. Do you understand?"

I nodded quickly, my eyes fixed on the floor.

He whooped me then, the belt snapping against my legs as I tried to stay still. The punishment wasn't unexpected, but it still stung—physically and emotionally. When it was over, he walked away, muttering under his breath about how he couldn't understand why I acted the way I did.

JJ, who had been watching from the doorway, gave me a knowing look. His expression wasn't one of sympathy or guilt. Instead, it was a subtle smirk, a silent reminder that this was how things were. This was my role in the house—to take the blame, to bear the punishment.

The rest of the day passed in a blur. My legs still stung from the whooping, but I forced myself to move through the motions—eating lunch, tidying up, and pretending everything was fine. JJ didn't mention the missing money or the punishment. He acted like everything was normal, like nothing had happened.

I envied his ability to move on so easily, to brush off things that stayed with me for days.

As I lay in bed that night, I couldn't stop replaying the day in my head. The laughter from the morning felt like a distant echo, overshadowed by the weight of the punishment and the lies I had told. Two days of normalcy had been too much to hope for.

This was my life. A fragile balance of fleeting moments of peace and the constant undercurrent of fear and tension. I closed my eyes, wishing for sleep to come quickly, knowing I'd need all the strength I could muster to face the next day.

CHAPTER 24: SOUND OF MERCY

Thursday began like any other summer day, the oppressive heat settling over the neighborhood as JJ and I played outside. The sun was bright and relentless, casting harsh shadows across the cracked pavement. The familiar sounds of summer—cicadas buzzing in the distance, the faint hum of a lawnmower, the occasional bark of a dog—filled the air, but I barely noticed. My focus was on keeping up with JJ, following his lead as I always did, because that's what kept things calm.

JJ was in a surprisingly good mood that morning. We tossed a ball back and forth, his laughter ringing out every time I fumbled a catch or stumbled over my feet. For a little while, it felt almost normal. I let myself believe that maybe today would be a good day.

That illusion shattered when JJ spotted the kitten.

He froze mid-throw, his eyes narrowing as he stared at something beneath one of the neighbor's cars. "What's that?" he said, his tone sharp with curiosity.

I followed his gaze, squinting to see. Under the car, half-hidden in the shadows, was a tiny kitten. Its fur was dusty and matted, and it looked too small to be out on its own. It crouched low to the ground, its green eyes wide with fear as it let out a soft, pitiful meow.

JJ's lips curled into a grin, and a chill ran down my spine. I knew that grin too well. It was the same grin he wore when he wanted to see something break.

"Leave it alone, JJ," I said, my voice trembling. I tried to keep it steady, but the unease in my chest was growing. He ignored me, crouching down and reaching under the car. The kitten backed away, its tiny body pressing against the wheel, but JJ was faster. His hands shot out and grabbed it by the scruff of its neck. He stood up, holding it out in front of him like a prize.

"Look at this little thing," he said, laughing. "It's so scrawny."

"Put it down," I said, my voice rising. "It's just a baby. Don't hurt it, JJ. Please."

He turned to me, his grin widening. "Relax, Tess. It's just a dumb cat."

I wanted to grab the kitten, to take it and hide it somewhere safe, but I was frozen. My feet felt like they were glued to the pavement, and my heart pounded in my chest.

JJ started walking toward the neighbor's backyard, where the fence separated their yard from ours. I followed him, panic bubbling up inside me. The neighbor's two rottweilers were already barking, their powerful bodies pacing back and forth along the fence. They were on high alert, their ears perked up, their eyes locked on JJ.

"JJ, no!" I screamed, tears already welling up in my eyes. "Don't do it! Please!"

He glanced back at me, his expression calm and smug, like this was nothing more than a game to him. "Let's see how long it lasts," he said casually.

"Stop it! Stop, JJ! I'm begging you!" I cried, my voice breaking. "Please don't!"

But he didn't stop. With a flick of his wrist, he tossed the kitten over the fence.

The barking turned ferocious in an instant. The high-pitched scream of the kitten cut through the air, a sound so sharp and raw that it made my whole body seize up. I turned away, squeezing my eyes shut and covering my ears, but I couldn't block out the sounds—the growls, the yelps, the horrible crunching. The kitten's cries faded quickly, replaced by the triumphant barks of the rottweilers.

When it was over, the silence felt deafening. I slowly uncovered my ears, my body trembling as I turned back toward JJ. He was standing there, watching the fence with a satisfied look on his face.

"What's wrong, Tess?" he asked, his tone mocking. "It's just a stupid cat."

But it wasn't just a stupid cat. It was a life. A small, helpless life that he had snuffed out for no reason other than his own amusement. Something inside me shattered in that moment, something I didn't even know was holding me together.

I turned and ran, tears streaming down my face. I didn't stop until I reached my room, where I crawled under the bed and pressed myself against the wall. The wooden floor was cool against my skin, but it did nothing to soothe the storm raging inside me. I sobbed into the quiet, my chest heaving as I tried to make myself as small as possible.

JJ's laughter echoed faintly in the distance, growing softer as he stayed outside. It was a cold, cruel sound, one that I couldn't escape no matter how hard I tried. I buried my face in my hands, wishing I could disappear.

The hours dragged by as I stayed under the bed, refusing to come out. The sun dipped lower in the sky, casting long shadows across the room. I stared at the slats of the bed frame above me, my mind blank except for the image of the kitten's wide green eyes. I couldn't shake it. I couldn't stop hearing its cries.

When Dad came home, his voice carried through the house, breaking the heavy silence. "Where's Tess?" he asked, his tone curious but unconcerned.

I didn't move. I stayed under the bed, my breathing shallow as I listened to JJ's voice in the distance, answering casually as if nothing had happened. "She's in her room," he said. "Probably asleep or something."

I wanted to tell Dad what JJ had done. I wanted to scream and cry and make him see how cruel JJ could be. But I stayed where I was, silent and still. What was the point? No one ever stopped JJ. No one ever saved me.

All I could think about was Friday. Grandma was coming to get me, and the thought of being anywhere but here was the only thing keeping me together. I didn't know how much longer I could endure this. JJ's cruelty seemed to grow every day, and I felt like I was slipping further and further into a darkness I couldn't escape.

I closed my eyes under the bed, holding onto the fragile hope that tomorrow would come quickly. If I could just make it to Friday, maybe—just maybe—I'd find a little peace.

CHAPTER 25: ROAD TO RESPITE

I sat on the couch, my knees pulled to my chest, watching the clock tick down the minutes. My stomach twisted with a nausea that had nothing to do with hunger. I hadn't eaten breakfast. I hadn't said much of anything all morning. Every tick of the second hand felt like a countdown to something I wasn't sure I could trust.

Barbara must have noticed. She glanced at me from the kitchen, wiping her hands on a dish towel. "You feeling okay, Tess?"

I nodded, forcing my voice steady. "Yeah."

She didn't push, just hummed in response before turning back to whatever she was doing.

Across from me, JJ sat at the table, chewing his cereal obnoxiously, letting the spoon clink against the bowl with every bite. He hadn't said anything yet, but I could feel him watching me, waiting.

Finally, he leaned back in his chair, stretching lazily. "You excited?" His voice was casual, but his eyes were sharp.

I didn't answer.

JJ smirked. "You should be. It's your funeral, after all."

The air in the room felt suffocating. I wrapped my arms around myself, staring down at the floor, willing the time to move faster.

And then, the low rumble of an engine outside. Grandma's van.

I shot up so fast my legs wobbled beneath me. My bag was already packed, sitting by the front door. I grabbed it without a second thought, my fingers tightening around the straps.

Barbara chuckled from the kitchen, oblivious to the panic twisting inside me. "Guess she really is excited."

JJ stretched again, yawning, but his smirk never left.

"Yeah," he muttered. "Real excited."

I didn't look at him. I couldn't.

Dad met me at the door, pressing a folded bill into my palm. "Give fifty to your grandma," he instructed. "The rest is yours."

I nodded, barely registering the words, my heart hammering against my ribs. He pulled me in for a brief hug, his embrace warm but fleeting, like everything about him. "Be good, alright?"

I forced a small nod.

Barbara gave a quick wave from the porch, already moving on to something else in her day.

I climbed into the van, my fingers gripping the seatbelt before I even had it buckled. The tension in my chest didn't ease until I heard the soft click of the door shutting behind me.

Grandma's hands were steady on the wheel as she put the van into drive.

I stared straight ahead.

I didn't look back.

The ride from LA to Riverside always felt long, but today, I wished it would stretch on forever. The van's familiar hum vibrated through my seat, the rhythm of the tires against the road a steady drumbeat beneath me. Majesty, the youngest of my older brothers, hopped out of the passenger seat when we stopped for gas, stretching like he had been the one driving. He was nine, short for his age but full of boundless energy, always darting from one place to another. Fortune, my seven-year-old sister, climbed out after him, gripping a small toy in her hand.

They were the only two of my siblings who had come along. The rest—too old, too uninterested—had stayed behind, letting us younger ones enjoy the trip.

"Tess!" Grandma's voice was warm as she reached for me, pulling me into a tight hug the moment I stepped out. The scent of lavender surrounded me, the familiar softness of her embrace undoing something inside me. For the first time all week, I felt safe.

Before we got back on the road, I dug into my pocket, pulling out the bill my dad had given me. I unfolded it carefully and handed fifty dollars to Grandma. "Dad said to give this to you."

She smiled, slipping it into her purse. "Thank you, baby." Inside the gas station, I wandered toward the coolers, the bright blue label of Fiji water catching my eye. It was expensive, the kind of drink Barbara would roll her eyes at, but I grabbed one anyway.

When I got back in the van, I twisted off the cap, taking a long sip before sighing in satisfaction. "This is so good."

Majesty turned to me, raising an eyebrow. "It's just water."

Fortune giggled, shaking her head. "Yeah, Tess, get off your high horse. It's not special."

I rolled my eyes but didn't argue. I liked Fiji water. It was mine.

Grandma's voice cut through the teasing as she pulled back onto the road. "Let her enjoy it," she said, her tone light but firm. "Y'all are always picking on her."

I shot Grandma a grateful smile.

The rest of the ride was filled with games and laughter. We played "I Spy," taking turns guessing things outside the window. "I spy with my little eye, something green," Majesty said, grinning mischievously.

"The trees!" Fortune guessed, her voice eager.

"Nope," he replied, drawing out the suspense.

"The grass?" I offered, looking out at the patches of green along the highway.

"Yeah," he said finally, nodding. "But it's brown in some places. Y'all were close."

We laughed and moved on to storytelling. Fortune told us about her class project, how she'd made a paper-mâché volcano that had erupted with baking soda and vinegar. Majesty talked about playing kickball at recess and how he had slid into home base, ripping his pants in the process.

When it was my turn, I shared about being the only five-year-old in the school play and how I got to play a lead role because I could read all the lines. Grandma listened intently, glancing at me in the rearview mirror with pride.

By the time we reached Grandma's house, the sun was dipping low in the sky, casting long shadows across the neighborhood. Her small, cozy home came into view, its front yard dotted with wildflowers and the faint outline of the porch swing swaying gently in the breeze.

"Here we are," Grandma announced as she parked the van. The three of us piled out, stretching our legs and grabbing our bags from the back. The air in Riverside felt different—calmer, quieter. It was like stepping into another world, one where the weight of everything I'd left behind in LA didn't feel so heavy.

Inside, the smell of something baking filled the house. Grandma had prepped the oven before she left, and the scent of warm cinnamon and apples made my mouth water. I set my things down in the corner and joined Fortune and Majesty in the living room, where they were already pulling out board games.

For the first time in days, I felt a flicker of peace. Being here, surrounded by Grandma's love and the simple joys of my siblings' company, made it easier to forget. I didn't know how long it would last, but for now, it was enough.

CHAPTER 26: OUTSIDER LOOKING IN

The next morning, I reached for the Fiji water I had saved from the day before. I twisted the cap off and took a sip, savoring the crisp taste. Before I could finish, Majesty and Fortune burst into laughter.

"You really drank that?" Majesty said, his voice dripping with mock surprise.

I frowned, lowering the bottle. "What's so funny?"

"We put toilet water in it," Fortune said with a smirk, her giggles bubbling over.

My stomach turned as I stared at the bottle in my hand. Their laughter filled the room, loud and teasing, and I couldn't tell if they were serious or just trying to get under my skin.

"Y'all are disgusting," I said, setting the bottle down and glaring at them.

"Relax, it's a joke," Majesty said, rolling his eyes. "You're so gullible."

It was annoying, sure, but maybe this was just sibling banter—normal stuff that brothers and sisters did. It wasn't like the torment I was used to back home. They teased me, but they didn't hit me or threaten me. I could handle this.

But then Fortune leaned closer, her tone turning sharp. "You're not even our real sister anyway. You're adopted."

"Yeah," Majesty chimed in. "You don't even belong here."

Their words stung, even though I tried not to let it show. I forced a shrug, keeping my face neutral. "Whatever," I said quietly. "Y'all are dumb."

Deep down, I told myself this was just what siblings did—teasing, poking, pushing boundaries. It hurt, but it was better than the hell hole I was used to. At least here, the pain didn't come with bruises.

By Saturday, the tension had eased. Grandma sent us outside to enjoy the day, her voice ringing through the house: "Y'all better not be in here when the sun's shining!"

We grabbed our bikes, and I quickly realized mine had a flat tire. The other kids started pedaling down the street while I pushed my bike along, trying to keep up. We passed by the small neighborhood bike shop, where a man was working on a rusty old bicycle out front.

"You need air in that tire?" he called out, noticing me struggling.

I nodded shyly. "Yes, sir."

"Bring it over," he said, smiling. "Let's get you fixed up."

I pushed my bike toward him, watching as he crouched down and filled the tire with air. He handed it back to me with a kind smile. "There you go, all set. No charge."

"Thank you," I said softly, my voice barely above a whisper. His kindness caught me off guard, and for a moment, I felt a small flicker of warmth.

I pedaled back to catch up with Majesty and Fortune, who were already riding around with the other neighborhood kids. The street was alive with laughter and the sound of wheels skimming over the pavement. Kids were playing tag, tossing balls, and racing their bikes up and down the block.

Fortune had found a group of girls her age, and they were laughing together, their voices high and cheerful as they huddled in a circle. I hung back, watching from a distance. She didn't invite me to join them, and I didn't expect her to. Fortune had a way of showing off, of making sure I knew she could boss me around if she wanted to. It annoyed me, but it didn't surprise me.

I tried not to care that I wasn't invited, but deep down, I wished I was. Not necessarily with her, but with someone. Anyone.

Instead, I pedaled my bike aimlessly, circling the block and pretending I was fine. I smiled when I passed the group of kids playing tag, hoping one of them would invite me to join. But they didn't. I was just a stranger to them, the awkward new kid who didn't know how to jump into their games.

I wished I wasn't so socially awkward.

It wasn't just shyness—it was the fact that I felt like I didn't belong in their world. The things they talked about—friends at school, boys they had crushes on, funny moments from their favorite TV shows—felt so far removed from my reality. Their biggest worries seemed so small compared to mine. How could I relate to kids who didn't understand what it was like to be me?

I watched from the sidelines, feeling the gap between us grow wider with every laugh I wasn't a part of. I wanted to join, to fit in, but I didn't know how. It was easier to stay on my bike, circling the neighborhood and pretending I didn't care.

When we got back to Grandma's house later that day, the smell of dinner greeted us at the door. The familiar scent of fried chicken and cornbread wafted through the air, pulling me out of my thoughts. Grandma was in the kitchen, humming softly to herself as she stirred a pot on the stove.

"How was your day, babies?" she asked, glancing up with a smile.

"Good," Fortune said quickly, launching into a story about the girls she played with and how they had come up with a new dance routine.

Majesty followed with his own tales of racing the boys in the neighborhood and how he almost won. They didn't ask about my day, and I didn't offer much. "It was fine," I said simply, slipping into my chair at the table.

As we ate dinner, I felt the weight of the day settle over me. I didn't mind being alone most of the time—it was safer that way—but today, for some reason, it felt heavier. Still, I reminded myself that this was better than the alternative. Better than being back in LA, where I had no peace at all.

Even in moments like this, when I felt like an outsider, I tried to hold onto that thought. At least here, I could breathe.

CHAPTER 27: DEFYING GRAVITY

Monday came, and the house felt quieter than usual. Majesty and Fortune were still in school, but only for one more week. Summer break was so close I could almost feel it in the air, the anticipation buzzing just beneath the surface. Even if I was out of school, if they werent there was more quiet pondering moments of reflection than I wanted.

Majesty was in homeschool, though, because he couldn't stop getting into fights. His temper was as quick as a match strike, and his fists usually followed. Grandma said he just needed guidance, but I wasn't so sure. Majesty thrived on chaos, but he was brilliant when it came to working with his hands. He could build or fix just about anything.

Fortune, on the other hand, was in second grade. She'd been held back because she couldn't read, and I always believed that the teasing from our older siblings about her struggles had something to do with how she treated me. It was like she carried their words with her, storing them up until she could let them loose on someone else—usually me. I understood it, in a way, but it still stung.

That day, Fortune was home early for her tutoring session. I could hear her in the living room with Grandma and the tutor, the soft murmur of voices punctuated by Fortune's frustration as she struggled with a sentence. It was a familiar sound, one that felt almost like the backdrop of our days. I stayed outside, where Majesty was working on his latest invention.

The backyard was dusty and worn, the grass patchy and dry in places. A chain-link fence separated us from the alley, and an old shopping cart sat in the middle of the yard, surrounded by tools and scraps of metal. Majesty crouched beside it, his hands moving quickly as he adjusted something on the frame. He didn't notice me at first, too focused on his work.

"What are you doing?" I asked, stepping closer.

He glanced up briefly, a grin spreading across his face. "Making a rocket."

I raised an eyebrow. "Out of a shopping cart?"

"Yep," he said, turning back to his project. "You'll see. It's gonna be awesome."

Majesty had somehow managed to attach a motor to the cart, rigging it up with a battery and a steering mechanism he'd pieced together from parts he'd found in the alley. It was messy—held together with duct tape, zip ties, and sheer determination—but it looked functional.

"You think it's gonna work?" I asked, skeptical but intrigued.

"Of course it's gonna work," he said confidently. "I'm not done yet, though. Hand me that wrench."

I picked up the wrench from the pile of tools and handed it to him, watching as he tightened a bolt with quick, precise movements. He was in his element, completely focused, and it was hard not to admire the way his mind worked.

When he finally finished, he stood up and wiped his hands on his shorts. "Alright," he said, stepping back to admire his creation. "Let's test it."

The cart was rough-looking, its frame scratched and worn, but the motor hummed quietly as Majesty pushed it toward the hill behind our backyard. The hill wasn't steep, but it was long enough to build up some serious speed. I followed him, my excitement growing despite myself.

"You wanna go first?" he asked, motioning to the cart.

I hesitated, eyeing the contraption warily. "Is it safe?"

He laughed. "Of course it's safe. I built it."

That didn't exactly fill me with confidence, but I nodded anyway. "Okay."

He helped me climb into the cart, adjusting the seat so I could reach the steering handle. It felt wobbly, the frame creaking slightly under my weight, but Majesty didn't seem worried. He climbed in behind me, his grin as wide as the sky.

"Alright, you ready?" he asked.

"Not really," I admitted, gripping the handle tightly.

"Too bad," he said, laughing as he kicked the brake loose.

The cart lurched forward, the motor kicking in as we began to roll down the hill. At first, it was slow, the wheels rattling against the uneven pavement. But then gravity took over, pulling us faster and faster until the world around us blurred. The wind whipped against my face, and I screamed—not out of fear, but out of exhilaration.

"Turn left!" Majesty shouted, laughing as the cart wobbled dangerously close to the fence.

I yanked the steering handle, and the cart veered left, narrowly missing a patch of broken glass on the pavement. We screamed and laughed, the rush of speed making everything else fade away.

As we hit the transition from cement to grass, the cart bounced and jolted, finally skidding to a stop near the bottom of the hill. For a moment, we sat there, catching our breath, our faces flushed with adrenaline.

"See?" Majesty said, grinning as he climbed out of the cart. "Told you it'd work."

I laughed, shaking my head. "You're crazy."

"Yeah," he said, shrugging. "But you had fun, didn't you?"

I couldn't argue with that. For a little while, everything felt simple—just two kids in a backyard, defying gravity and forgetting the weight of the world. It wasn't perfect, but it was enough.

CHAPTER 28: A SUMMER NIGHT WITH GRANDMA

The sun had dipped below the horizon, leaving behind a hazy orange glow that melted into the deepening blue sky. The air was still warm, but the worst of the day's heat had faded, replaced by a soft breeze that whispered through the trees.

Grandma and I sat on the front porch, rocking slowly in the chairs she kept just outside the door. The old wooden boards creaked beneath us, the sound mixing with the faint hum of crickets and the occasional bark of a dog from somewhere down the street.

Dinner had been long over, and Fortune and Majesty were inside, their laughter muffled through the screen door. But out here, it was just us—just me and Grandma and the quiet night stretching out in front of us.

She sipped on her sweet tea, the ice clinking softly in the glass as she turned her gaze toward the sky. "You see them stars up there, baby?" she asked.

I followed her line of sight, my eyes landing on the clusters of stars that had begun to appear, twinkling like tiny, scattered diamonds.

"Yeah," I murmured.

She smiled, the kind of smile that held something deeper behind it—memories, maybe, or wisdom I wouldn't understand just yet. "Used to sit out here when I was your age, looking at them same stars," she said. "Made me feel like I was part of somethin' bigger. Like even if the world around me felt small, there was more out there waitin' for me."

I didn't say anything, just let her words settle over me like the warmth of the night air.

She took another slow sip of her tea, then looked over at me, her expression soft. "Your daddy told me you been gettin' in trouble."

My stomach tensed, and I glanced down at my lap. She didn't sound mad. Not like Barbara, not like my dad when he was disappointed. She just sounded... like Grandma.

"Said you been caught stealin'," she continued, her voice gentle. "But you know what I told him?"

I shook my head.

"I told him I ain't never had to worry about that with you."

I swallowed hard, unsure of what to say.

Grandma leaned forward, resting her elbows on her knees. "Now, I ain't sayin' what you did was right, but I know a thing or two about why people do what they do. And I know you, Tess. I know you wouldn't take what you didn't feel like you had to."

I bit my lip, staring hard at my hands.

She reached out, placing her warm, weathered hand over mine. "Whatever's goin' on, baby, you don't have to carry it all by yourself."

The words lodged themselves deep in my chest, heavy and unfamiliar. I wanted to believe her. I wanted to tell her. But I couldn't.

So I just nodded.

Grandma didn't push. She just gave my hand a squeeze before leaning back in her chair, rocking slowly once again. "One day," she said softly, "you're gonna get where you're meant to be. Just hold on till then."

I swallowed the lump in my throat and tilted my head back to look at the stars again.

Maybe she was right.

Maybe I just had to hold on.

That night, I lay awake in bed, staring at the ceiling.

Grandma's words repeated in my head over and over.

"The truth don't change just because you're afraid to say it."

I didn't know if I'd ever be brave enough to tell the truth.
But for the first time, I let myself wonder—
What if?
What if someone did believe me?
What if telling the truth could actually change something?
I wasn't ready yet.
But maybe, one day, I would be.

CHAPTER 29: THE COUSINS COME TO VISIT

The house buzzed with energy as soon as my cousins arrived. The front door swung open, and suddenly the quiet of the past few days was replaced with loud voices, laughter, and the sound of sneakers stomping across the wooden floors.

It wasn't just Majesty, Fortune, and me anymore. Now there were three more of us—our cousins, all older, all bigger, all full of energy that filled every corner of Grandma's house.

The yard became a battlefield of play-fights, chases, and shouted dares. The dry grass crunched beneath our feet as we raced across it, the summer heat pressing down but doing nothing to slow us down.

We started with play-fighting, throwing light punches and testing each other's strength. It was fun at first—until the punches got a little too hard, the shoves a little rougher. My cousins were stronger than me, their bodies heavier, their laughter sharper as they knocked me off balance over and over again.

I stumbled backward after a particularly hard shove, landing on the ground with a thud. My elbow scraped against the dirt, stinging.

"Come on, Tess," one of them teased, grinning down at me. "You gotta toughen up!"

I forced a laugh, brushing the dirt off my arms as I stood back up.

We moved on to Blind Man's Bluff, tying a bandana around the eyes of whoever was "it" and spinning them around before letting them stumble after the rest of us. When it was my turn, I struggled, reaching blindly as their laughter echoed around me.

"You're so slow, Tess!" someone shouted, darting out of reach just before I could tag them.

I swung my arms, trying to catch someone, anyone, but they were all too fast. The bandana was hot against my skin, the sun beating down, and the frustration built in my chest like a knot.

By the time we switched to tag, I was already worn out. And of course, I was almost always "it."

I chased them, but they were faster. Stronger. Always just out of reach.

I pushed myself harder, my legs burning as I sprinted after them, but no matter what, I couldn't catch them.

I wasn't fast enough. I wasn't strong enough.

"You're too slow, Tess!" one of them yelled, laughing as they dodged me again.

I stopped running.

My chest heaved. My face was hot.

I was done.

"I'm not playing anymore," I said, my voice flat. I turned on my heel and walked toward the house, ignoring their protests.

"Aw, come on, Tess! Don't be a sore loser!"

I ignored them.

Inside, the air was cool, a stark contrast to the heat outside. I went straight to the kitchen and poured myself a glass of water, the cold glass sweating in my hands. I sat at the table, staring down at the surface, listening to their muffled voices through the window.

They were still playing.

They hadn't even noticed I was really gone.

I told myself it didn't matter.

It wasn't like I was ever part of their world anyway.

CHAPTER 30: A QUIET MOMENT WITH GRANDMA

The house was quieter now. The cousins had left, and the playful chaos of the past few days had settled into something softer—a calm before the storm.

I sat at the kitchen table, tracing circles on the worn wood with my fingertip as Grandma hummed a gospel tune under her breath. She moved around the kitchen with ease, flipping cornbread in the skillet, the scent of butter and warmth filling the air.

"You're awful quiet, baby," she finally said, turning to look at me.

I shrugged. "Just thinking."

She sat down across from me, wiping her hands on a towel before folding them neatly on the table. "What's on your mind?"

I didn't know how to answer that. Not really. If I told her the truth—that I wasn't ready to go back home, that I was afraid, that I felt like I was walking into a trap—I wasn't sure what she would do.

So I just said, "I don't want summer to end."

Grandma smiled knowingly, reaching over to tuck a stray curl behind my ear. "I know, baby," she said. "You always get like this when it's time to go home."

I looked down at my hands. "It's just… it's easier here."

She nodded, understanding in her eyes. "I know. But Tess, you are strong. You have always been strong."

I felt my throat tighten. I didn't feel strong. I felt small.

Grandma leaned forward, her voice softer now. "I want you to remember something. No matter where you are, no matter what's going on, you are never alone. You hear me? You got people who love you. People who see you."

I swallowed hard and nodded.

She reached for my hand and gave it a squeeze. "And one day, baby… one day, you're gonna get out of there for good. You won't always be stuck."

Her words hit deep, settling somewhere inside me like a seed planted in the dark. I didn't know when—or if—that day would come. But I wanted to believe her.

I needed to believe her.

CHAPTER 31: FINAL DAYS OF SUMMER

The last few days before I left felt different.
The air was thick with that late-summer heaviness, the kind that made the whole world feel slow. The sun set earlier now, the golden light stretching long across the pavement as if even the sky was trying to hold on to the last bits of summer.
I spent most of my time outside, riding my bike up and down the street, trying to soak in as much of this place as I could. I watched Fortune and Majesty run off to play with the neighborhood kids, but I didn't follow.
I didn't feel like belonging today.
Instead, I just watched. Watched the way laughter seemed to come so easy to them. Watched the way the world felt safe in a way that I knew wouldn't last.
At night, I lay awake, staring at the ceiling, listening to the crickets outside. I imagined myself stretching summer out longer, making it last forever. What if I just never left? What if I hid under Grandma's bed when she

drove back, stayed behind, and disappeared into the comfort of this place?

But time didn't stop. It never did.

And soon enough, the last night arrived.

CHAPTER 32: WELCOME BACK TO HELL

The ride home from summer vacation felt unbearable. The days I had spent at Grandma's house were like a reprieve, a pocket of safety and warmth that I knew I wouldn't have again for months. The van felt smaller on the way back, the air heavier, and the laughter of my siblings—Fortune and Majesty—only made it worse. They played road games in the backseat, their voices light and carefree as they called out things they spotted on the road.

"I spy something green!" Fortune exclaimed, giggling when Majesty guessed wrong.

"It's the sign!" she said triumphantly, clapping her hands.

I stared out the window, silent, watching the world blur past. Their games felt meaningless to me. How could they laugh and joke when I was leaving behind the only place I ever felt safe? Every mile brought me closer to something I didn't want to face, something they couldn't understand.

The way back felt far too short.

When we finally pulled into the driveway, the house loomed in front of me like a shadow. The weight of it pressed down on my chest, making it hard to breathe. My stomach twisted as I looked at the doorway, where JJ was already standing, his arms crossed and a smug smile on his face. He didn't say anything, but he didn't have to. His presence was enough to send a chill down my spine.

I couldn't do this. I wasn't ready.

Tears welled up in my eyes as the car came to a stop. Before I knew it, I was crying, the sound spilling out of me in loud, uncontrollable sobs. "I don't want to go back!" I screamed, my voice cracking as I clutched the seat. "I'm not ready! Please don't make me go back!"

My siblings turned to look at me, their faces a mix of confusion and discomfort. Fortune's mouth opened slightly, her eyes wide, while Majesty frowned and shook his head. To them, I must have seemed crazy, overdramatic, even childish. They didn't know. They couldn't know.

"Why's she acting like that?" Fortune asked, her voice low as if she didn't want to be heard.

"Beats me," Majesty muttered. "She's always doing the most."

Grandma got out of the car, and I could hear her speaking to my parents, who had come outside to greet us. "She's just upset about leaving," Grandma said, her voice calm but tired. "She'll be fine once she settles in." "She'll see you again for Easter break," my dad said, waving off my tears like they were nothing more than a tantrum. "Right, Tess? You'll be fine."

But I wasn't fine. I stumbled out of the van, my legs shaky beneath me, and threw my arms around Grandma. "Please don't leave me," I whispered, my voice breaking. "Please."

She hugged me tightly, her arms warm and steady. "It's gonna be okay, baby," she said softly. "You'll see me soon. Easter's not that far away."

Her words didn't bring me any comfort. Easter felt like a lifetime away, and I couldn't imagine enduring another day in this house, let alone months. I clung to her until my dad pulled me away, his grip firm but not unkind. "You're fine," he said again, guiding me toward the house. "Stop all this crying."

JJ stood in the doorway, his smile growing wider as I approached. He didn't say anything, but the look on his face said it all: Welcome back to hell.

I froze for a moment, my legs refusing to carry me inside. My parents gave me a gentle shove, ushering me into the house as if I were a reluctant guest. I glanced back at the van, wishing I could run back to it, back to Grandma, back to safety. But the door closed behind me, sealing me in.

The house felt smaller, darker, colder than I remembered. The walls seemed to close in around me, suffocating me with memories of everything I had tried to forget over the summer. JJ's laughter echoed faintly from down the hall, a haunting reminder that he was waiting. Waiting for the first opportunity to make me regret ever coming back.

I sat on the edge of my bed that night, staring at the wall as tears slid silently down my cheeks. The house was quiet, but the silence was heavy, filled with the weight of what I knew was coming. My heart ached for Grandma's house, for the laughter, the warmth, the safety.

This was going to be a long school year.

CHAPTER 33: A CRUEL WELCOME HOME

When we got back home, I eventually calmed down. The tears dried, though the heaviness in my chest remained. I tried to push it aside as the evening wore on, focusing on the small semblance of normalcy that followed. We sat in the living room as a family, the TV playing one of Dad's favorite old Western movies. The room smelled faintly of popcorn, though I hadn't touched mine. My siblings laughed at the cheesy action scenes, and Dad chuckled every now and then, his focus glued to the screen.

I sat quietly, trying to blend into the background. My mind was still at Grandma's house, replaying the warmth of her hugs, the sound of her humming in the kitchen, the safety I'd felt in her presence. Here, it felt like all of that had been stripped away, leaving me exposed and raw.

Then JJ broke the peace.

"Hey, Dad," he said, leaning forward with a grin that sent a chill down my spine. "Watch this."

I froze, my heart pounding as JJ turned to me. "Tess!" he called out, his tone sharp and commanding. "Come here."

I hesitated, my body tensing as I glanced at Dad. He seemed curious but not concerned, his eyes flicking between us. I stood slowly, my legs heavy as I walked toward JJ.

"Tell Dad who your daddy is," JJ said, his grin widening.

My stomach dropped. "I'm not saying that," I muttered, my voice barely above a whisper.

JJ's expression darkened, his eyes narrowing. "Say it," he said firmly, his voice low and threatening. "Tell him."

I glanced at Dad, silently pleading for him to intervene. He looked confused, maybe even slightly amused, but he didn't stop JJ. "What's he talking about?" Dad asked, his tone light, as if this were some kind of joke.

"I'm not saying it," I repeated, my voice shaking.

JJ leaned closer, his grin fading into a cold, hard stare. "Say it," he said again, his voice barely audible but filled with menace.

I swallowed hard, the lump in my throat making it difficult to breathe. My palms were sweaty, my heart racing. I didn't want to say it—I didn't want to give him that power—but the thought of what he might do if I refused terrified me more.

"JJ," I said finally, my voice cracking. "JJ's my daddy."

Dad's expression shifted from curiosity to disbelief. He sat up straighter, his eyes narrowing as he looked at JJ. "What the hell are you teaching her to say?" he asked, his voice stern.

JJ shrugged, leaning back in his seat as if nothing had happened. "It's just a joke," he said casually. "She knows who her real daddy is."

"Well, don't joke like that," Dad said firmly, shaking his head. "That's not acceptable."

But that was it. No anger, no punishment. He dismissed it as just another one of JJ's antics, something he didn't want to deal with.

I stood there, feeling disgusted and betrayed. I wanted to scream, to tell Dad that it wasn't a joke, that JJ was always like this, but the words caught in my throat. JJ glanced at me, his grin returning, as if he knew exactly what I was thinking. I turned and went back to my seat, my hands clenched into fists.

Later that night, after the house had quieted and everyone had gone to bed, my door creaked open. I didn't have to look to know who it was. The familiar sound of JJ's footsteps made my stomach churn as he stepped into the room and closed the door behind him.

"Hey, Tess," he said, his voice soft but sharp. "You know no one wants you here, right?"

I stayed silent, my body frozen under the covers.

"Grandma doesn't want you. She couldn't wait to get rid of you at the end of the summer," he continued, his words like poison dripping into my ears. "And Dad? He only keeps you around so he doesn't have to pay child support. You think he actually cares about you?"

Tears pricked my eyes, but I refused to let them fall. I turned my head away, pressing my face into the pillow to hide the trembling of my lips.

"And Fortune and Majesty?" he added, his tone cruel. "They hate you, too. You're not really their sister. You're just the extra kid no one wanted."

His words stabbed at me, each one hitting harder than the last. I wanted to scream at him, to tell him he was lying, but deep down, I wasn't sure if he was. The things he said played into my worst fears, the thoughts that already lingered in the back of my mind.

JJ crouched beside the bed, his face inches from mine. "You know I'm the only one who tells you the truth, right?" he whispered, his voice calm and cold. "No one else is gonna tell you how it really is."

He stood up and left, his footsteps fading down the hall. I lay there in the dark, my body shaking with silent sobs. His words echoed in my head, louder than my own thoughts, drowning out everything else.

This was my first night back, and I already felt like I was drowning. The safety I had felt at Grandma's house was gone, replaced by the cold, suffocating reality of home. I hugged my pillow tightly, closing my eyes and wishing for sleep to take me away, even if just for a little while.

CHAPTER 34: THE LAST ATTEMPT

The house was quiet, but not the peaceful kind. It was the kind of silence that felt heavy, like a storm pressing down before it hit. The kind of silence that suffocates.
I sat on my bed, staring at the door, my hands curled into fists on my lap. JJ's words still clawed at my mind, over and over, refusing to let go.
"Nobody wants you. Grandma couldn't wait to get rid of you. Dad only keeps you to avoid child support."
Was it true?
I didn't want to believe it. But when you hear something enough, when it's repeated like a chant in the dark, it starts to feel real.
I needed to hear something different. I needed proof that JJ was wrong.
Dad was in the living room, sitting at the table with the TV humming in the background. He had his plate in front of him, the smell of reheated food lingering in the air. I hesitated in the hallway, watching him. He looked relaxed, comfortable in his own world. A world I never felt part of.

I swallowed hard and stepped forward.

"Dad?" My voice came out small, barely above a whisper.

He barely looked up, his focus still on the screen. "What?"

I shifted on my feet, my nails digging into my palm. This was my chance. I had to say it.

"JJ says... he says nobody wants me." I let the words hang between us, my heart pounding so loud I was sure he could hear it. "That Grandma only takes me for the summer because she has to. That you only keep me because of child support. That nobody—" My voice broke, and I bit down hard on my lip to stop it from shaking.

Dad sighed. Not the kind of sigh that meant concern—the kind that meant annoyance.

"Tess," he said, rubbing his temple. "Why are you always starting something?"

I blinked. "I—I'm not—"

"You are." His voice hardened. "You're always in something. Always causing trouble. Always playing the victim."

I took a step back. My stomach turned.

"JJ says you stole from me."

I froze.

Dad finally looked at me, his eyes sharp. Expecting a lie. Expecting an excuse.

"You're a thief, Tess. You've been stealing from me all school year. And you think I'm gonna believe you over JJ?"

His words punched through me harder than any belt ever had.

My throat burned. "I—I didn't—"

He slammed his hand against the table. "Stop lying!" His voice thundered through the room, rattling the walls, rattling me.

I flinched, my body shrinking back, my breath coming in short, shaky bursts.

My father stood up, towering over me. "You always lie. You lie about stealing. You lie about why you get in trouble. You lie about everything."

I shook my head, my voice barely a whisper. "I'm not lying."

That was it. That was the end of the conversation. In his eyes, JJ could do no wrong. And I could do nothing right.

I stood there, feeling the weight of it settle over me.

I wasn't a daughter. I wasn't even a child.

I was the problem.

I turned and walked away before he could say anything else. I didn't run. I didn't cry. I just left, my feet carrying me back to my room as if on their own.

When I closed the door behind me, I let out a breath I didn't realize I was holding. My hands shook.

JJ had been right.

Dad didn't want me. He didn't believe me. He never would.

I climbed onto my bed, curling my knees to my chest.

The room felt smaller, the walls pressing in, trapping me.

For the first time, I understood.

I was alone.

No one was coming to save me.

No one even believed I needed saving.

That was the moment something inside me shut off.

I wouldn't try again.

I wouldn't ask for help.

I wouldn't expect it.

I had to figure this out on my own.

CHAPTER 35: FADING INTO THE PAGES

The next day, I barely spoke. I barely moved.

I drifted through the morning like a ghost, quiet and unseen. The house hummed with its usual sounds—Barbara moving through the kitchen, the TV murmuring in the background, JJ's presence lurking just beyond my line of sight. But it all felt distant, like a world I wasn't really part of anymore.

I stayed in my room.

The walls felt closer, the air heavier, but it was better than being out there. Better than pretending.

My diary sat open in my lap, the pages crinkled from how often I had flipped through them. It was the only place that felt safe. The only place I could be honest, where my words weren't questioned, where my voice wasn't drowned out by JJ's lies or my father's indifference.

I picked up my pen, my fingers trembling slightly, and let the words pour out.

I don't feel like I exist here.

I paused, staring at the sentence, then kept writing.

I walk through this house, and no one really sees me. They see a thief. They see a liar. They see trouble. But they don't see me.

My grip on the pen tightened.

Maybe I should just stop trying. Maybe if I stay quiet enough, small enough, they'll forget I exist completely. Maybe that would be easier.

The words blurred, the ink smudging slightly under my fingertips. I wasn't crying—I had run out of tears long ago.

I set the diary aside and reached for a book. Any book. Reading was the only thing that worked. The only thing that could make the noise in my head shut up. I wasn't Tess when I was reading. I wasn't trapped in this house, under the weight of JJ's threats or Dad's disappointment.

I was somewhere else.

In a world where kids weren't ignored. Where the underdogs fought back. Where people cared enough to see what was happening right in front of them.

I turned the page, letting the words consume me. The room faded. The house faded. The world around me blurred into the background.

And that's how it went.

Every day, I disappeared a little more.

I spoke less. I felt less.

I became less.

JJ didn't notice—he didn't need to. He had already won.

Dad didn't notice either. No one did.

And maybe that was the point. Maybe if I could just shrink small enough, I wouldn't have to feel anything at all.

So I let it happen.

I let the books swallow me whole. I let the words wrap around me like armor.

Because if I was going to survive this house, I had to stop being me.

CHAPTER 36: WORDS THAT SAVED ME

The final few days of summer drifted by like a slow-moving cloud, heavy with the weight of what was to come. I spent most of my time with my nose buried in books, escaping into worlds that felt safer and brighter than my own. The words on the pages were like brushstrokes, painting vivid pictures in my mind and pulling me far away from the confines of the house.

I devoured every story I could get my hands on, each one a lifeline that carried me through those last days of freedom. I loved the way the words etched themselves into my brain, how the sentences seemed to dance and twist, creating lives and adventures so different from my own.

I didn't just read the stories—I lived them. In my mind, I wasn't Tess, the unwanted girl stuck in a house full of tension and fear. I was the brave protagonist, fighting dragons, solving mysteries, uncovering hidden treasures. I overcame every obstacle, defeated every villain, and came out stronger on the other side.

Sometimes I'd close the book and stare at the ceiling, imagining myself as one of the characters. What would it be like to be bold and fearless, to have people rallying behind me, believing in me? What would it feel like to win?

The house was quiet most of the time. JJ spent his days outside, hanging out with friends or tinkering with whatever project had captured his interest that week. Dad and Barbara were busy, their focus on each other and the newness of their marriage. Fortune and Majesty were off doing their own thing, leaving me to my books. I didn't mind being alone. The silence gave me space to lose myself in the pages, to forget about the looming return to school and the heavy feeling that came with it. I read stories about kids like me—underdogs, outsiders, the ones who didn't quite fit in. But unlike me, they always found a way to rise above. They were brave in ways I couldn't be, clever in ways I only wished I was. I clung to their victories like they were my own, each page a small reminder that maybe, just maybe, I could find a way to overcome my own challenges someday.

One afternoon, I sat by the window with a book in my lap, the sunlight streaming in and warming the worn carpet beneath me. The sound of laughter floated in from outside—JJ and his friends, no doubt—but I tuned it out, focusing instead on the story in my hands.

The protagonist was standing up to a bully, their words sharp and powerful, their courage unwavering. I felt my heart race as I read, my fingers gripping the edges of the book. I could almost hear their voice, feel the strength in their stance.

And for a moment, I let myself imagine it was me. What would I say if I had the chance? If I could stand up to JJ, to Dad, to the world that always seemed to weigh me down? The thought lingered, bittersweet and fleeting, before I pushed it aside and returned to the safety of the story.

Books were my escape, my armor, my lifeline. They let me pretend, even if only for a little while, that I was more than the scared, uncertain girl sitting in a quiet house waiting for the school year to start. They gave me hope, in their own way, that maybe one day I'd find my own story worth telling.

Books weren't just stories to me—they were worlds I could step into whenever my own became too heavy to bear. Each page was a portal, and with every turn, I could feel myself slipping further away from the confines of my reality. I didn't just read the words; I absorbed them, letting them flow through me like a current, carrying me somewhere else entirely.

I loved the way a good story made me feel like I wasn't alone. The characters, with all their flaws and fears, felt real to me in a way that people didn't. I could see myself in them—the scrappy underdog fighting against the odds, the quiet kid longing to be heard, the hero who found courage in the darkest moments. They became my friends, my confidants, my silent teachers. Sometimes, when the house was too quiet or when JJ's presence loomed like a storm cloud, I'd imagine myself as one of the protagonists. I'd close my eyes and see myself standing tall, my shoulders squared, my voice steady and strong. In my mind, I wasn't scared of anything—not JJ, not my parents' indifference, not the ache of being unwanted. I was bold, clever, unstoppable.

One story in particular stuck with me—a tale about a girl who was overlooked and underestimated, dismissed by everyone around her. But she had a secret: a fire inside her that no one could extinguish. She faced bullies and monsters, doubters and liars, and she never gave up. By the end of the book, she had saved her world, her strength and determination shining like a beacon.

I must have read that book five times that summer. I dog-eared the pages, underlined my favorite passages, and even copied down a quote into my diary: "Even the smallest light can burn brighter than the sun." I read that line over and over, letting the words sink in. I wanted to believe it—that even I, as small and insignificant as I felt, could burn bright enough to make a difference.

When I read, the world around me faded. The sounds of the house—the creak of the floorboards, the hum of the air conditioner, JJ's voice carrying down the hall—blurred into the background. I could spend hours lost in a book, forgetting everything else. I'd become the adventurer navigating uncharted lands, the detective piecing together clues, the warrior standing tall in the face of danger. In those moments, I wasn't just escaping; I was rewriting myself.

But closing the book was always the hardest part. The moment I turned the last page, reality came rushing back, like a tidal wave crashing over me. The walls of my room, the weight of the silence, the distant sound of JJ laughing—they all reminded me of where I really was. And as much as I tried to hold onto the courage I'd felt while reading, it always seemed to slip away, leaving me with nothing but the ache of wanting to be someone else.

Still, I kept reading. Because even if the stories didn't change my life, they changed me. They made me believe, even for just a moment, that there was more to the world than what I saw around me. And maybe, just maybe, there was more to me, too.

CHAPTER 37: THE WEIGHT OF THE FIRST DAY

The morning of the first day of school began with the same suffocating heaviness that had settled over me all summer. My stomach churned as I got dressed, the newness of my clothes feeling foreign and stiff against my skin. The fabric scratched at my arms, another small discomfort in a day I already dreaded.

JJ had already left by the time I shuffled into the kitchen. The front door had slammed behind him minutes earlier, a final punctuation to his presence. The silence that followed was a temporary relief.

Barbara stood at the counter, stirring sugar into her coffee, her mind somewhere else. "You ready?" she asked without looking up.

I nodded, though my throat felt too tight to speak.

She grabbed her keys, taking one last sip of coffee before motioning for me to follow. "Let's go."

The car ride was quiet. The hum of the engine filled the space between us, but we didn't talk. She didn't ask how I felt about school, and I didn't offer anything. I kept my hands folded in my lap, staring out the window as we drove past familiar streets.

The school came into view too quickly. My chest tightened as Barbara pulled into the drop-off lane.

"Alright, have a good day," she said, her tone neutral.

I hesitated before reaching for the door handle. "Okay," I mumbled, stepping out onto the sidewalk.

I didn't look back as she drove off.

The moment I stepped into Ms. Walker's classroom, I felt small.

The room was neat—too neat. Desks were arranged in perfect rows, and the bulletin boards were bright and organized, covered with class rules and schedules. There was something intimidating about the way everything was in its place, as if Ms. Walker's expectations had already been set before we even walked in.

She stood at the front of the classroom, posture straight, arms crossed. Her presence filled the room before she even spoke. "Find your seat quickly, please," she said, her voice sharp but even.

I kept my head down as I found my desk, my name printed in careful, looping letters on a laminated tag. I slid into my seat and ran my fingers over the smooth surface, grounding myself in the coolness of the desk beneath my palms.

The other kids chatted, their energy buzzing in the air, excitement filling the space I couldn't seem to fit into. They were laughing, exchanging stories about summer vacations, sleepovers, and birthday parties. I didn't have anything to add.

When it was time for introductions, Ms. Walker went around the room, having each of us share our name and something we liked.

"I'm Tess," I said when it was my turn, my voice barely above a whisper. "And… I like reading."

Ms. Walker gave a short nod before moving on, but the moment still lingered in my chest.

The rest of the morning dragged on, filled with lectures about classroom expectations, rules, and routines. Ms. Walker's no-nonsense approach became clear almost immediately—there was no room for distractions or drifting off.

But I couldn't focus.

My mind drifted, caught between the world outside the classroom and the one I had left at home. The ache in my chest never fully settled, and every time I glanced up at Ms. Walker, I felt the weight of her watchful eyes.

"Tess," she called on me suddenly. "Can you answer the question?"

My heart dropped.

I blinked down at my notebook, the lines of my page empty.

"I... I don't know," I mumbled.

Her lips pressed into a thin line. "Pay attention," she said, her tone sharp but controlled. "This isn't the time to daydream."

I nodded quickly, heat burning my cheeks as the other students turned to look at me. The humiliation settled in my stomach like a stone.

By recess, I needed space.

I walked to the far edge of the playground, away from the clusters of kids who were already forming groups. The air was filled with bursts of laughter, the sound of jump ropes smacking the pavement, the squeak of sneakers against the blacktop.

They belonged here.

I didn't.

I sat on the grass, picking at the blades between my fingers, watching the other kids from a safe distance. They talked about summer vacations—trips to Disneyland, family road trips, new pets. I had nothing to share, nothing that made sense in their world.
I stayed quiet, letting their voices blur into background noise.

When we returned to the classroom, Ms. Walker handed out worksheets. The questions stared up at me, but I couldn't bring myself to focus. I traced the edge of my paper with my fingertip, my mind elsewhere.
"Tess."
I flinched at the sound of my name. Ms. Walker stood beside my desk, her sharp eyes scanning my blank worksheet.
"You're capable of more than this," she said quietly, her voice firm but not unkind. "I expect better from you."
I swallowed hard and nodded, but the words sank into me like a stone.
I wanted to tell her I was trying. That I couldn't shake the weight sitting heavy on my chest. That it wasn't about effort—it was about survival.
But I stayed silent.

Because I knew she wouldn't understand.

The day crawled to an end.
As the final bell rang, I exhaled a breath I hadn't realized I was holding. I stuffed my papers into my backpack and slipped out of the classroom without looking back.
Barbara was already waiting in the car when I stepped outside. I climbed in, my bag feeling heavier than it had that morning.
"How was it?" she asked, her voice casual.
"Fine," I said, staring out the window.
She nodded, but she didn't press for details.
I watched the school fade into the distance, my reflection staring back at me in the window.
School was supposed to be an escape, a place where I could leave the chaos of home behind.
But it was becoming clear—there was no escaping it.
Not here. Not anywhere.

CHAPTER 38: UGLY TESS

It didn't take long for Ms. Walker and me to become enemies—not that she would have said it out loud, but I could see it in the way her eyes narrowed every time I spoke. The classroom felt colder with her in it, her no-nonsense approach leaving no room for the things I couldn't control: my need to talk, to move, to distract myself from the chaos in my head.

Day after day, I found myself in trouble. It didn't matter what I did—whether I whispered to a classmate, tapped my pencil too loudly, or blurted out an answer without raising my hand—Ms. Walker was always there to correct me. Her frustration was palpable, and it seemed to feed the whispers of the other kids, their eyes darting toward me every time she scolded me.

"Stop disrupting the class, Tess," she snapped one morning when I had giggled at a joke another kid whispered to me.

"I wasn't disrupting!" I argued, the words spilling out before I could stop them.

She placed her hands on her hips, her expression stern. "Do you think arguing with me makes this better?"

I glared at her, my hands clenched into fists beneath my desk. "Maybe it's better than sitting here being bored." The room went silent, all eyes on us as Ms. Walker's face tightened. "Out," she said sharply, pointing toward the door. "Go back to Ms. Smith's class. Now."
I grabbed my things and stormed out, my cheeks burning with humiliation. It wasn't the first time she had sent me to Ms. Smith, and it wouldn't be the last.

In Ms. Smith's classroom, everything felt different. Her voice was calm, her presence gentle in a way that made me feel less like a problem and more like a person. She didn't ask questions when I walked in with a note from Ms. Walker, just smiled and motioned for me to sit at the back of the room.
I didn't feel brave enough to look her in the eye, but the way she treated me made my chest ache with something I couldn't quite name. It wasn't kindness exactly—it was more like she saw me, really saw me, even when I didn't want to be seen.
"You can stay here as long as you need," she said quietly as she handed me a worksheet. "Just do your best."

But when the day ended and I had to go back to Ms. Walker's class, the cycle started all over again.

The tipping point came one afternoon when I was tapping my pencil against the desk, trying to keep my hands busy while Ms. Walker explained a math problem on the board.

"Tess, stop that," she said without turning around.

I froze for a moment, but as soon as she turned back to the board, I started tapping again. I wasn't trying to be defiant—I just couldn't seem to stop.

She spun around, her expression sharp. "That's enough," she snapped. "Why are you always acting so ugly?"

Her words hung in the air, sharp and cutting. The other kids snickered, and I felt their eyes on me, their judgment weighing me down like a stone.

After that, it was like Ms. Walker had given them permission to say what they had been thinking all along. "Ugly Tess," they whispered under their breaths, their voices mocking. "Ugly Tess."

I tried to ignore them, but the words burrowed into me, their weight unbearable. That's when I started roaring.

Every time Ms. Walker spoke, I made a loud, guttural sound, like an animal trying to scare off a predator. It was the only thing I could think to do to drown out their laughter, to make myself feel like I had some kind of power, even if it was ridiculous.

"Tess, stop that," Ms. Walker said, her voice sharp.

I didn't stop.

"Tess!" she yelled, slamming her hand on the desk. "Enough!"

I roared louder, the sound ripping out of me like a scream.

That afternoon, Ms. Walker sent me to the hallway with my desk, dragging it out herself while the class watched.

"If you can't act like a student, you won't sit in my classroom," she said firmly.

I sat there, staring at the empty hallway, my chest heaving with anger and humiliation. My mind raced with questions I couldn't answer. Why did she hate me so much? Why couldn't I stop acting out? Why did everything feel so impossible?

The next day, Ms. Walker barely looked at me, her frustration clear in every stiff movement. But then something happened—something small, but enough to make her pause. During quiet reading time, I accidentally dropped my book, the loud thud drawing everyone's attention.

She turned to scold me, but her words faltered when she saw my face. I wasn't angry or defiant this time—I was crying, silent tears streaming down my cheeks as I picked up the book and held it tightly to my chest.

For a moment, her expression softened. She opened her mouth as if to say something, but then closed it again, turning back to her desk.

The moment passed, but it stayed with me. Maybe, just maybe, she had seen something more in me than just the troublemaker she always sent away.

By the end of the week, the whispers of "Ugly Tess" had faded, but the damage was already done. I felt smaller, weaker, more invisible than ever. Ms. Walker seemed exhausted by me, and I hated her for it. But more than that, I hated myself for being everything she said I was.

CHAPTER 39: SEEING THROUGH THE WALLS

(Ms Walkers POV)

The cafeteria was quieter than usual during the teachers' lunch period. Most of the staff sat in small clusters, chatting softly or grading papers as they ate. Ms. Smith sat at the far end of the room, her lunch neatly arranged in front of her. She had just opened a book when Ms. Walker approached, her tray balanced in one hand.

"Do you mind if I join you?" Ms. Walker asked, her tone polite but weary.

Ms. Smith smiled warmly, closing her book and motioning to the seat across from her. "Of course. How's the second week of school treating you?"

Ms. Walker sighed as she set her tray down. "Tess," she said, her voice heavy with frustration. "That girl is wearing me out."

Ms. Smith's expression softened. "What's she been doing now?"

"She's disruptive, defiant, constantly acting out," Ms. Walker said, shaking her head. "Yesterday, she started roaring in the middle of my lesson. Roaring, Ms. Smith. I had to send her to the hallway with her desk."

Ms. Smith let out a small sigh, her eyes thoughtful. "And how did she look when you sent her out?"

Ms. Walker paused, frowning as she thought back. "Angry. Frustrated. But… there was something else, too." She hesitated, her voice lowering. "Defeated, maybe? Like she just gave up."

Ms. Smith nodded knowingly. "I've seen that look before," she said softly. "It's not just you, you know. Tess has been struggling for a long time."

Ms. Walker leaned forward slightly, her frustration giving way to curiosity. "How did you get through to her? She's constantly in trouble in my class, but she seems calmer when she's with you."

Ms. Smith hesitated for a moment, choosing her words carefully. "It's not about getting through to her," she said finally. "It's about understanding that there's more to her behavior than what you see in the classroom. Tess is… carrying a lot."

"What do you mean?" Ms. Walker asked, her brow furrowing.

Ms. Smith lowered her voice, glancing around the room to ensure no one was listening. "I believe Tess is being abused at home," she said quietly.

Ms. Walker's eyes widened, her expression a mix of shock and concern. "Abused? Are you sure?"

Ms. Smith nodded. "I've suspected it for a while. The way she flinches when someone raises their voice, the exhaustion in her eyes, the way she acts out—it's all there. I've tried to report it before, but Tess won't stick to her story. She always backs out, says she was lying, or blames herself."

"Why?" Ms. Walker asked, her voice tinged with disbelief.

Ms. Smith sighed, her face heavy with sadness. "Fear, most likely. Loyalty to her family, maybe. She's still a child, Ms. Walker. She doesn't want to get anyone in trouble, and I think part of her believes it's her fault."

Ms. Walker sat back, processing the information. "What can we do?" she asked finally. "If she won't stick to her story, how can we help her?"

"The only thing we can do is build trust," Ms. Smith said firmly. "I've spent over a year trying to show her that I'm someone she can rely on, someone who won't judge or dismiss her. It's not easy, but it's the only way."

Ms. Walker was silent for a moment, her gaze distant as she thought about Tess's behavior in her class—the roaring, the defiance, the way her eyes filled with tears when she thought no one was looking. "I had no idea," she said quietly. "I've been so frustrated with her, but... I never thought there might be a reason behind it."

Ms. Smith reached across the table, placing a hand on Ms. Walker's arm. "You're not alone," she said gently. "It's easy to miss the signs, especially when a child acts out the way Tess does. But now that you know, you can approach her differently."

Ms. Walker nodded slowly, determination flickering in her eyes. "I'll try," she said. "I don't know if she'll trust me, but I'll try."

The next day, I noticed something different in Ms. Walker. It was subtle at first—the way her voice softened when she corrected her, the way she seemed to hesitate before handing out a punishment. I couldn't quite put my finger on it, but it made her uneasy.

During math, I fidgeted in my seat, her pencil tapping against the desk. I expected the usual sharp reprimand, but when Ms. Walker looked up, her expression wasn't angry. Instead, she sighed and walked over to my desk.

"Let's try to focus, okay?" Ms. Walker said, her voice calm. "I know you can do this."

I froze, her pencil still in her hand. She stared at Ms. Walker, unsure of what to say. The usual anger wasn't there, and it threw her off balance. "Okay," I mumbled, lowering my eyes.

Throughout the day, I kept noticing the changes—small, subtle things that made her feel... different. Less like a problem and more like a person. But the kindness made me uneasy. I didn't trust it. What if it was a trick? What if Ms. Walker was just trying to get her to slip up?

That night, as I laid in bed, couldn't shake the feeling that Ms. Walker was starting to see through her walls. And as much as I craved the kindness, it terrified me. Because if Ms. Walker dug too deep, she might uncover the truth—and I wasn't sure she was ready for that.

CHAPTER 40: BREAKING THE WALLS

The changes in Ms. Walker were subtle at first. She didn't suddenly become warm or overly friendly, but her sharp edges seemed softer. She corrected me less harshly, her tone calm instead of biting. I wasn't sure what to make of it. Part of me wanted to believe she was different, but another part, the part that braced for disappointment, couldn't let go of the suspicion that it was all a trick.

One afternoon during reading time, I sat at my desk, quietly flipping through a book, when a boy behind me whispered loud enough for others to hear, "Why's she always so weird?"

My heart sank. Heat spread across my cheeks, but before I could react, Ms. Walker's voice cut through the classroom.

"Ben," she said firmly, setting her book down and looking directly at him. "That's not how we treat people in this classroom. Do you understand?"

Ben's face turned red, and he mumbled an apology. The other kids fell silent, the atmosphere shifting as Ms. Walker's words hung in the air.

"Tess, would you like to share what you're reading with the class?" she asked, her tone lighter but still kind.

I hesitated, gripping the edges of the book. My first instinct was to say no, but the way she looked at me—it wasn't mocking or impatient. It was almost… encouraging.

Slowly, I stood up, my knees trembling as I turned to face the class. "It's about a girl who finds a treasure map," I said quietly, holding up the book. "She's… brave."

"That sounds amazing," Ms. Walker said with a smile. "Thank you for sharing, Tess. I think we could all use a little bravery, don't you?"

The tension in the room eased, and I sat back down, feeling a flicker of something I hadn't felt in a long time: pride.

A few days later, during group work in math, I sat by myself while the other kids clustered into groups. I watched them laugh and talk, their voices blending into a blur of noise that made my stomach twist. I was used to working alone, but today, it stung more than usual.

"Tess," Ms. Walker called from the front of the room. "Why don't you join Sarah and Emily's group?"

I froze. Sarah and Emily were two of the quieter girls in the class, the kind who never teased me but also never went out of their way to talk to me. I hesitated, glancing toward them nervously.

Ms. Walker walked over, crouching slightly to meet my eye level. "You're great at math," she said softly. "I think they could really use your help."

Reluctantly, I nodded, picking up my workbook and moving to their table. At first, we didn't say much, and I stayed quiet, afraid of saying the wrong thing. But as we worked through the problems, something shifted.

"Wait," Sarah said, pointing at my paper. "How did you figure that out?"

I blinked, surprised. "I… just counted backward."

"That's smart," Emily said with a small smile. "Can you show me how you did it?"

Hesitating, I leaned forward, explaining the steps. For the first time, I didn't feel like an outsider. I felt… included.

Ms. Walker continued creating moments like these, moments that chipped away at my walls. During a spelling activity, when another boy whispered, "She's probably gonna mess it up," Ms. Walker immediately shut him down.

"Tommy," she said, her tone firm. "That's not acceptable. We lift each other up in this classroom, not tear each other down."

She turned to me and said, "I believe in you. Take your time."

I didn't mess up. I spelled the word correctly, my heart pounding with a mixture of relief and pride as Ms. Walker nodded approvingly.

The biggest shift came during an art project. Ms. Walker paired me with Olivia, who was known for being shy but kind. I felt nervous at first, unsure of how to connect, but Ms. Walker stopped by our table, offering gentle encouragement.

"You two are both so creative," she said. "I can't wait to see what you come up with."

As we worked, Olivia started talking about her favorite cartoons. I surprised myself by chiming in, mentioning a show I used to watch at Grandma's house.

"No way," Olivia said, her eyes lighting up. "I love that one!"

For the rest of the project, we talked and laughed quietly, finding common ground in a way I hadn't expected. By the end of the day, Olivia waved at me as we packed up our things. It was a small gesture, but it made my chest feel warm.

That night, as I lay in bed staring at the ceiling, I thought about the way Ms. Walker had stepped in when the kids teased me, the way she encouraged me to participate, the way she gently nudged me toward making friends. It felt strange, like something shifting inside me.

I still didn't trust Ms. Walker completely—part of me was still waiting for the other shoe to drop—but I couldn't deny that things felt… different. For the first time, I wasn't just the troublemaker. I was something more.

CHAPTER 41: THE CONFESSION

It happened during math, an ordinary moment that turned into something I couldn't take back. The classroom was quiet except for the sound of pencils scratching against paper as we worked through a series of word problems. Ms. Walker moved through the rows, her sharp eyes scanning our work, occasionally pausing to correct someone or offer guidance.

I sat at my desk, gripping my pencil tightly. My mind wasn't on math. It was on the weight of everything I'd been carrying—the teasing, the whispers, the things no one knew but me. The weight felt heavier than ever, pressing down on me like I was suffocating.

Ms. Walker stopped beside me. "Tess, are you finished?" she asked.

I looked up at her, the question hanging in the air for a moment. I wanted to say yes, to pretend everything was fine, to keep the words locked inside. But something about the way she looked at me—patient, steady, like she was actually waiting for my answer—made my throat tighten.

I hesitated. My grip on the pencil loosened. And before I could stop myself, the words spilled out.

"I have scars on my back."

The room fell silent.

Every head turned toward me, the weight of their stares pressing down harder than the words I'd just spoken. My chest tightened. I immediately regretted it. My heart pounded so hard I thought I might throw up.

Ms. Walker froze, her eyes widening slightly. I expected her to dismiss it, to tell me to focus on my math. But then, her expression shifted.

She crouched beside my desk and spoke in a voice so low only I could hear. "Tess," she said gently, "can you stay behind at recess? I'd like to talk to you."

The rest of the lesson passed in a blur. I kept my eyes on my desk, my breathing uneven. What had I done? What was going to happen now?

When the bell rang, the other kids rushed out to the playground, their laughter echoing down the hallway. I stayed behind, feeling trapped in my seat as Ms. Walker pulled up a chair and sat down beside me.

She didn't ask right away. Instead, she sat with me in silence for a moment. Then, in a calm, steady voice, she said, "Tess, you don't have to be afraid. I promise, you're not in trouble. But I need to know—what did you mean?"

I clenched my hands in my lap, my fingers twisting together. My body screamed at me to lie, to brush it off, to tell her I had just been joking. If I said too much, if I let her in, I knew things would change.

But hadn't I wanted that?

Didn't I need that?

I took a deep breath, then let it out shakily. "I didn't mean anything," I whispered, but even I didn't believe it.

Ms. Walker stayed quiet for a long moment. Then she leaned in slightly, her eyes searching mine. "Tess, you don't have to do this alone. If something's wrong, I want to help."

The lump in my throat grew bigger, and my vision blurred. I wanted to trust her. I wanted to believe that she meant it. But I had spent so long pretending I was fine, that part of me wasn't sure I knew how to stop.

But what if this was my only chance?

My hands trembled as I reached for the hem of my shirt. Slowly, I lifted it just enough for her to see.

I heard her sharp intake of breath, and when I turned back around, her eyes were glassy with unshed tears.

"Oh, Tess," she whispered, her voice thick with emotion. "I'm so sorry."

I dropped my shirt and looked down at my hands. My heart felt like it was going to burst, and I couldn't tell if it was from fear or relief.

"I'm going to help you," Ms. Walker said firmly. "You don't have to go through this alone anymore."

The rest of the day passed in a haze. Ms. Walker must have acted quickly because by the time the final bell rang, there were people waiting for me outside the classroom.

A woman with a clipboard. A man in a suit. Two police officers.

"Tess?" the woman said, crouching slightly to meet my eye level. "My name is Ms. Harper. We're here to talk to you about what you shared with your teacher. Can we do that?"

I nodded hesitantly, my heart pounding as I followed them into an empty classroom. They asked me questions—about the scars, about my home life, about JJ and my dad and everything I'd tried so hard to keep hidden. I answered as best as I could, my voice shaky but honest.

Afterward, they brought my dad into the room. His face was pale, his eyes red as he sat down across from me. I had never seen him cry before, but the tears were there, streaming down his face as he looked at me.

"I didn't know," he said, his voice breaking. "Tess, I didn't know."

I didn't say anything. I didn't know what to say.

"I'm so sorry," he said, his hands trembling as he reached for mine. "I should have seen it. I should have protected you."

For a moment, I wanted to believe him. I wanted to believe that things could be different, that this was the start of something better. But deep down, I knew it wasn't that simple.

They told me I couldn't go home.

Not yet.

They said it wasn't safe, that they needed to make sure I was protected. My dad cried harder when they said this, his hands covering his face as he shook his head.

When it was time to leave, I was walked off school grounds with Ms. Harper by my side, the police officers trailing behind us. My classmates stared from the playground, their eyes wide with curiosity and confusion. I avoided their gazes, my heart pounding as I said goodbye to Ms. Walker and Ms. Smith—the teachers who had made this day happen.

"Thank you," I said quietly, my voice barely above a whisper.

Ms. Walker placed a hand on my shoulder, her expression full of emotion. "Take care of yourself, Tess. You're stronger than you think."

Ms. Smith nodded, her eyes shining with tears. "We're proud of you."

As I climbed into the car, I looked back one last time. My dad stood there, watching me leave, his shoulders slumped in defeat.

Epilogue

They didn't tell me exactly where I was going—just that it would be somewhere safe. Somewhere without JJ. Somewhere where I wasn't afraid to go to sleep at night. For the first time in my life, I wasn't running from something—I was running toward something new.
And maybe, just maybe, that was enough.

Author Biography – Ness Turner

Ness Turner is a storyteller, entrepreneur, and survivor who uses her voice to bring light to the unspoken realities of childhood trauma. As the **founder of Bounce Brothers Inflatables and TurnerRound Logistics**, she has built businesses centered on resilience, creativity, and transformation—values that echo throughout her writing.

With a deep passion for storytelling, Ness writes with raw honesty and emotional depth, giving voice to those who have felt silenced. Her debut memoir, **At the Tender Age of Five**, is a powerful testament to survival, strength, and the journey toward healing.

Beyond her businesses and writing, Ness enjoys spending time with her family, creating engaging content, and finding ways to inspire and uplift others. Through her work, she hopes to remind readers that even in the darkest of times, hope is never truly lost.